START WITH NO

START
WITH
NO

The Negotiating Tools That the Pros Don't Want You to Know

JIM CAMP

CROWN
BUSINESS
NEW YORK

Copyright © 2002 by James R. Camp

Published by Crown Business, New York, New York.
Member of the Crown Publishing Group, a division of Random House, Inc.

www.randomhouse.com

CROWN BUSINESS is a trademark and the Rising Sun colophon is a registered trademark of Random House, Inc.

Printed in the United States of America

Design by Susan Maksuta

Library of Congress Cataloging-in-Publication Data

Camp, Jim.
    Start with no : the negotiating tools that the pros don't want you to
  know / by Jim Camp.—1st ed.
    1. Negotiation in business.   I. Title.

HD58.6.C36 2002
658.4'052—dc21   2001047742

ISBN 0-609-60800-2

10 9 8 7 6 5 4

First Edition

To my wife, Patty

Contents

START
WITH
NO

Introduction

Win-Win Will Kill Your Deal

HOW OFTEN OVER the past couple of decades have we read
or heard the phrase "win-win"? Thousands, I guess. Enough,
I know. The term has become a cliché in our culture, the only
acceptable paradigm for personal interaction of any sort. In business, its appeal rests on the proposition that no company has the
right to plunder a market just because it enjoys a position of
strength and dominance. We believe that a shared prosperity—a
win-win prosperity—is the sustainable one.

It all sounds so good, what stick-in-the-mud could possibly
disagree that win-win is the model to use in negotiation? Well, I
disagree. Based on my nearly twenty years of experience as a negotiation coach, I believe win-win is hopelessly misguided as a
basis for good negotiating, in business or in your personal life or
anywhere else. This book and my system should be viewed as a

rejection of win-win and all its kind. Of the various ideas in my system that I could have chosen as my title, I selected *Start with No* expressly to emphasize my profound disagreement with win-win, which implicitly urges you to get to *yes* as quickly as possible, by almost any means necessary. Such negotiating is the worst possible way to get the best possible deal. In fact, it will get you killed.

Maybe you work for one of the many companies around the world that proudly display those shiny win-win trophies presented to the sales team by their largest customers. That's right, actual trophies, each and every one of which is testimony to a *failed* negotiation. Testimony to a negotiation conducted without discipline and without a system. Testimony to a negotiation conducted by naive amateurs, to be perfectly blunt. I think it's great that eight-year-old girls and boys receive trophies in their baseball and soccer leagues regardless of whether they were the champions that season. I think it's astonishing that top executives don't understand that it is precisely the win-win negotiations that are grinding their businesses into the ground. But this is often the case. I know, because many times I've walked right past the win-win trophy case on my way to meet the executives who want to hire me as a negotiation coach because things have gotten so bad.

"But so many deals have been negotiated on the basis of win-win! So many headlines, articles, books! It must work!" My answer is simple: The fact that a given deal was negotiated and signed tells me nothing at all. Who said this was a good deal, much less the *best* one? Just as the fact that the Cleveland Indians scored eight runs tells me something, but not enough, because the Yankees may have scored *nine,* so I need to know the final score in these so-called win-win deals.

And I do. I know that a certain worldwide delivery company became an industry juggernaut by negotiating deals with hundreds of small vendors across America that the company then abrogated in order to obtain leverage for a better deal—better for the delivery company, that is. Were those first deals good for the vendors? Just ask them. What about the second deals? Ask the vendors about these, too. I know that certain clothing retailers have made a specialty of squeezing vendors into signing pie-in-the-sky deals with production targets they cannot possibly meet. When they don't come through, the companies enforce the letter of the law, nullify the contracts, and then return in a month or so to renegotiate at the proverbial dime-on-the-dollar, because they now have all the leverage. Were those first or second deals good for the vendors? Just ask them.

When I became a full-time negotiating coach in the 1980s, after years of more informal tutoring, I didn't just say to myself, "Jim, there's always a niche for the contrarian in any field, so why don't you go challenge the win-win paradigm?" Nor am I a go-for-the-jugular tough guy who enjoys bullying people, as if this were the only alternative to win-win. The business world is certainly full of such individuals, and we will meet some of them in these pages, but I'm not one of them. No, I began to challenge win-win because I quickly learned that it's all too often win-*lose*. Make no mistake about it: a simply terrible but supposedly win-win deal is signed every minute in this country. The promise is just manipulation. It's all double-talk.

Think about the situation this way: If a company with a good product or service and with adequate resources goes bankrupt, which happens daily, what is likely to be *more* responsible for this fatality than poor negotiating with suppliers, customers, employees, *someone?* But even as the number of win-win losers grows and grows, the unwary are still legion. If I accomplish nothing in this book beyond alerting businesspeople to the dangers of win-win, I will have performed a valuable public service. I feel so strongly on this subject I'm now going to devote a couple more pages to it.

Some readers—I'm among them—tend to skim or even skip book introductions. Please don't do so this time. In order to understand my system, you *must* understand the dangers *inherent* in win-win.

They're Lying in Wait

I am not the first professional negotiator to understand the inherent weakness of the reigning philosophy. Not at all. Many, many corporate opportunists and shrewd negotiators in every field understand that a gung ho, win-win negotiator on the other side of the table is a sitting duck. In fact, one increasingly popular, high-level corporate strategy in negotiation commonly known in the business world by the acronym PICOS was developed for the *sole purpose* of defeating weak win-win negotiators.

This an instructive story, which I'll pick up in the early 1990s, when a man named Jose Ignacio Lopez de Arriotua was a main player in the procurement department for General Motors. (Many readers will remember Lopez for his subsequent highly publicized defection to Volkswagen in 1992 amid charges that he stole GM secrets. The federal government has indicted him for industrial espionage, but he's fighting extradition from Spain.) Lopez and his cohort at GM developed PICOS, or Program for the Improvement and Cost Optimization of Suppliers. (I've also seen it spelled out as Purchased Input Cost Optimization, so take your pick.) The advertised idea of this "costing method" was to help suppliers hold down their own costs in the design and production stage of the products they sold to GM. By holding down suppliers' costs, GM held down suppliers' prices and thereby GM's own costs.

So what could be wrong with helping suppliers hold down their own costs? That's win–win, isn't it? It sure was—for GM, because when the rhetoric was stripped away, "cost optimization" was a politically correct euphemism for bludgeoning suppliers into submission. It was nothing more or less than a diligent, sustained, extremely effective way for the giant automaker to drive down costs by putting the squeeze on its thousands of suppliers, no matter the result to them. If a supplier went belly-up or couldn't deliver under the negotiated terms, there was always another supplier who believed that it could somehow live with these prices. PICOS and its win–win rhetoric sounded good in theory, but it was and is devastating in practice for many businesses.

Today, several major business schools have developed similar programs for cost optimization or "supply systems management," as they are also labeled, and I imagine many others will follow suit, because GM and other large corporations have had great success with them. The business school that teaches the win–win mantra in a course on negotiation might also teach, right across the hall, a course in "supply system management" that's expressly designed to destroy the win–win model! Mindboggling.

Just a couple of weeks before writing this book I happened across an interview on one of Northwest Airlines's audio channels with the CEO of a new company that develops software for "interactive electronic commerce." This CEO was boasting about how the company's procurement software helps their clients "dominate their suppliers." That's the quote, and that's just the tip of the iceberg. The Net will facilitate the growth of huge buying cooperatives, multi*billion*-dollar initiatives that will allow competitors to combine their buying power in order to drive down suppliers' prices and add another tool to their cost optimization arsenal: "If your terms aren't good enough, we'll put it up for bid on the Net." I have no idea how this will all shake out in the years ahead, but I do know it represents more leverage for the big boys.

The Invitation to Unnecessary Compromise

What is the poison that resides at the heart of the big lie that is win-win? You've heard of the deadly stuff. It's called *compromise*. Many negotiators play the win-win game with an implicit invitation to debilitating early compromise on the part of their unwary adversaries, who are, in turn, almost *programmed* into this fatal mistake by the mantra of win-win. Those smooth-talking negotiators *don't* compromise, but they demand that you do. (In the case of corporate purchasing departments, I guess their compromise is that they're buying from *you* instead of from someone else.) And all the while, they put the happy face on their negotiations. GM acquired the deserved reputation of being a bully, so it and all the other big purchasing companies learned to be even more diligent in their use of win-win rhetoric, playing on our old-fashioned, all-American, Dale Carnegie instinct to win friends and influence people. They say, "Let's team up on this, *partner.*" They play on the time-honored American tradition of collective bargaining. In fact, almost every recent book on negotiation—many dozens, if not hundreds, including academic texts and popular paperbacks alike—structure their wisdom and advice around legally mandated collective bargaining in labor relations (the National Labor Relations Act of 1935): negotiating in good faith, give-and-take, compromise. In collective bargaining, a negotiator can be sent to jail for failing to bargain in good faith—for rejecting win-win, in effect. It should be no surprise that many win-win gurus in this country were educated and trained in this field.

In and of itself, tightly regulated collective bargaining is fine. So is generic "bargaining in good faith." Of course you want to bargain and negotiate in good faith. I insist on it with my clients. But when the tiger across the table says, "Now, Denise, Tom, you have to consider our legitimate interests here. We have to have a little good faith here, a little win-win," what is Denise and Tom's first thought? It's probably that they have to give up something if they need to sign this deal—and of course they do need to sign this deal, it's such a big one for their company. They have allowed themselves to be subtly manipulated into feeling responsible for the results reported to his boss by their adversary. They're nice people, so they compromise in order to help their adversary become a winner, too, though they have no idea what makes him a winner. When naive, eager-to-earn Denise and Tom are negotiating with a cunning tiger who has *also* read the win-win books, they are in terrible jeopardy.

Please remember this: The negotiators for many of the dominant multinationals are tigers. Most if not all of the great businessmen and businesswomen are tigers. I dare you to walk into the negotiating cage with them or their colleagues or a team of cost optimization negotiators while using one of the win-win textbooks as your bible. If you don't believe me, please check with suppliers for a certain worldwide delivery company and for certain retail clothing companies. Please check with smaller companies who deal daily with the giants of the Brave New Economy out on the West Coast. And I can assure you that negotiators in Saudi Arabia and Japan don't know about our American tradition of collective bargaining—or if they do, it's in order to take advantage of the negotiator who comes to their table with that mind-set. Was Ho Chi Minh playing win-win games in those fateful negotiations over Vietnam? I don't think so. But Richard Nixon and Henry Kissinger and their team were.

The furthest thought from Ho's shrewd mind was negotiating a "wise agreement," as defined in *Getting to Yes,* the leading win-win book on the market today. A quick look at that definition will be highly instructive. It reads: "A wise agreement can be defined as one that meets the legitimate interests of each side to the extent possible, resolves conflicting interests fairly, is durable, and takes community interests into account."

Sounds nice enough, but exactly who decides which interests are "legitimate"? In whose eyes are conflicting interests "fairly" resolved? And what does "to the extent possible" mean? And what does "durable" mean—that the agreement lasts a month, a year, or for the ages? And which "community interests" are we talking about? There are many of them, often in competition, one with the other (schools, labor, management, the environment, city hall—just for starters).

One more time: "A wise agreement can be defined as one that meets the legitimate interests of each side to the extent possible, resolves conflicting interests fairly, is durable, and takes community interests into account." In a perfect world, maybe, but in this one I hear "Taps" playing in the background. Compromise is implicit—almost explicit—within this definition. Of course, our hypothetical negotiators Denise and Tom *do* have to consider their adversary's "legitimate interests," once they figure out what they are, but this does *not* necessarily mean they need to give up a single dime.

Why in the world compromise before you're certain you have to? Sometimes you do, and that's fine, but often you don't, and that's better. The key point is that with the win-win mind-set, *you'll never know which it is.* Think carefully about this for a moment: Win-win and compromise are a defeatist mind-set from the first handshake. Negotiating under the banner of win-win, you'll have no way of knowing if you've made good and necessary decisions leading up to the compromise.

Maybe some readers are already thinking, "This Jim Camp approach sounds too cold-blooded for me. I *like* the idea of win-win. I believe it makes for a better, fairer world." Now I hear "Taps" playing not quietly in the background, but loud and clear. Let me illustrate with a quick, true story. Imagine that you are one of a small crew of young software hotshots in Silicon Valley and a Japanese firm offered to license your state-of-the-art technology for $400,000. You need some capital, and here's some nice capital. You guys and gals live on practically nothing, and this money might get you over the hump, and these investors are smart enough to think highly of your work and kind enough to go out on a limb for you. It's a good win-win deal, right? So this team thought. They were tempted to accept the initial offer before they were introduced to me, and I suggested a different approach because I found out that this Japanese firm that had pretended for six months that this $400,000 offer was all they could afford was actually a subterfuge group working on behalf of a major Japanese car manufacturer to buy American technology as cheaply as possible. Such "hit squads," as they're known, are notorious in Silicon Valley, and their equivalents op-

erate in every field of business, large and small, and usually under
the humanitarian guise of win-win. The final negotiated fee for
that crew's technology was $8 million. Why? Because that's what
it was worth. Win-win would never have netted what that technology was worth.

Maybe some readers are also already thinking, "But what
about that word 'adversary' you used earlier, Camp? I don't like
that. Negotiation isn't a war." No, it's not a war, and while I realize that the word "adversary" may carry confrontational conno-
tations, I define it as "respected opponent." You are negotiating
with a respected opponent. I employ the word "adversary"
mainly to counter the mushy idea that the folks on the other side
want to be your friend, and may even pretend to be your friend.

Sure win-win sounds good! That's exactly why it's so dangerous and why you have to be so careful. When negotiating over
the fence with your neighbor about what time you should fire
up the coals for the big barbecue, you might well get by with
win-win, but not against the tough, seasoned negotiators in the
outside world.

Emotion-Based versus *Decision*-Based Negotiation

It's crazy out there. In many, many corporations, the sales force
adheres to the win-win paradigm and therefore compromises at
every opportunity in its desperation to "get the business," while
the various purchasing agents and departments are well skilled in
one of the theories of supply systems management that are designed to take advantage of win-win vendors. Do the chief executive officers understand the contradiction here, the absurdity,

and do they understand that *both* the win-win and the PICOS paradigms are self-defeating? I wonder.

Here's a true story that perfectly proves my point. On one side of the negotiating table was a medium-sized company that sells a product vital to the high-tech world. I'll call this company Euphoric, Inc. On the other side of the table was a division of a giant multinational that supplies a chemical vital to Euphoric's product. I'll call this supplier Worldwide, Inc. In this negotiation, Worldwide approached Euphoric and requested a renegotiation of the contract for their patented chemical, which is petroleum based and therefore had become much more expensive to produce, given a worldwide increase in oil prices. Euphoric refused to renegotiate the contract. A deal is a deal, they said. In reply, Worldwide slowed down its shipment of the chemical, and without this chemical, Euphoric would have to shut down its line.

How much would Worldwide's request have added to Euphoric's unit cost? About fifteen cents. How much did Euphoric retail this unit for? A little over $2,000.

Those numbers are not typos. The battle was raging over a fifteen-cent increase in cost for a $2,000 product. What in the world could account for such blindness? It's very simple. Worldwide, like vendors everywhere, was so used to compromising at every opportunity in the name of win-win that they were afraid to insist on the justified premium for their patented product. Meanwhile, the purchasing folks at Euphoric were risking tens of millions of dollars in business because they, like purchasing departments everywhere, were blindly committed to taking advantage of win-win adversaries at every opportunity. Both sides were in an emotional box, committed to abstract theories of negotiation, and neither side made good decisions. In the end, Worldwide got its premium, because it was the best decision for both companies, but the negotiation was ridiculously long and involved and expensive.

This book is a refutation of all such *emotion*-based negotiating. As an alternative, I present for your consideration *decision*-based negotiating. In the end, I believe you'll agree with me that the difference between the two is clear and that the choice between the two is easy.

When I was in the air force, I learned, first in the classroom and then by practice in the cockpit, decision after decision, mistake after mistake, that I could not directly control the actions and decisions of my adversary, but I could, through trained habits, better manage my *assessment* of my adversary and make certain that it was accurate. With good decision-making skills, I had a chance at maintaining control of the situation and thereby achieving a beneficial outcome. Likewise, I couldn't absolutely control my emotions—no one can—but I could keep them under check, I could keep them from overly influencing my *actions,* with carefully constructed behavioral habits. This is precisely how the surgeon or any other practitioner learns his or her craft: through practice, study, making good and bad decisions, correcting the bad ones, more practice, more study, more decisions, more corrections.

I focused on what I could control—the means—not what I could not control—the end. The focus of this book is teaching you how to do the same during negotiation, because too many negotiators do just the opposite. They focus on what they *cannot* control—the end—while losing sight of what they *can* control—the means.

I like this analogy with baseball. Barry Bonds and Sammy

Sosa cannot control whether they hit a home run. After all, Bernie Williams may climb the wall and take it away, or the long fly may confront a jet stream that keeps the ball on the warning track. A lot of things can happen in the end, so Bonds and Sosa can only focus on the means to the end: putting a pure, sweet swing on the ball. They think only in terms of maintaining power and leverage in the process of the swing. If they think in terms of homers, they *lose* power and leverage by overswinging and lunging at bad pitches.

The analogy with a business negotiation is direct, which I realized almost from the first day I thought seriously about the subject, when helping a friend in California work out a small business deal. You cannot control the other party's actions and decisions—not directly—but you can control your assessment of your adversary's situation, and you can, with a great deal of work and discipline, control your own actions and decisions, and you can keep your emotions under check. My system teaches you how to control what you can control in a negotiation. When you do so, you can and will succeed (understanding that success sometimes means walking away with a polite good-bye).

My principle (and title), "Start with No," is based on the understanding that "no" is a decision. An early "yes" is probably a trick, and "maybe" is just that, maybe, and gets you nowhere. But "no" is a decision that gives everyone something to talk about, that helps you maintain control, as I'll explain in detail in chapter 3.

Another rule is "No Closing." But this is absurd, you may think. After all, "How to Close" is a more or less mandatory section of almost every negotiation book, so it has to be important. But I'm not playing games. Large deals, and even smaller ones, don't "close" in the usual sense of the term. They *come to-*

gether, through vision and decision, over weeks and months and maybe years. Moreover, if closing this deal is your goal, your preoccupation, maybe even your life's dream, then you're concentrating on what you *cannot* control and forgetting about what you can control. When negotiating with real pros, you'll pay the price in the end for this misguided behavior. In my system, you forget about winning and concentrate on the fundamentals of sound decision making.

At first encounter, some people—many, to be frank—are skeptical of these and other rules I use in my work, because they seem to fly in the face of conventional business wisdom. Some new clients have even been actively resistant, but after closer consideration, certainly after one trial negotiation, the great majority of these men and women are converted, because inviting the adversary to say "no" simply works. The "No Closing" rule simply works. Concentrating on what you can actually control in a negotiation—the means, not the end—simply works.

The so-called contrarian suddenly becomes common sense.

The Camp *System*

To repeat: Win-win is often win-*lose* because it invites unnecessary compromise, because it is *emotion*-based, not *decision*-based, and because it plays to the heart, not to the head. And one more thing: Win-win is not based on definitive principles; it's based on mush like the definition of a "wise agreement" I've already cited.

A win-win negotiation is not controlled in a clear, step-by-step way. That's just one reason win-win gets slaughtered in the real business world, again and again and again. I know CEOs who are proud of their deal making, but they have no discipline, no real basis for making their decisions. They're shooting from the hip under the assumption that everyone else is shooting from the hip. But some of their adversaries aren't. Some are shooting with a telescopic lens and the unwary win-win adversary is the target. It's not a fair fight.

Many readers will have heard Ross Perot's often-told story about the American who wants to buy a camel, pulls up at a tent with half a dozen camels staked in front, and asks the owner about one particular animal. The bedouin replies, "Oh, that's my son's camel, his pet. I couldn't sell that one." The American looks nonplussed, gets back into his Range Rover, and starts to drive off. The bedouin runs after him, shouting, "I thought you wanted to buy my camel!"

I agree with Ross Perot: Americans don't know how to negotiate! Okay, you ask me and Perot, how did these CEOs get to the top if they're such incompetent negotiators? Since win-win isn't a system and offers no real basis for judging those who "use" it, mediocrity flourishes without being detected. We all know there's a fair amount of mediocrity in American business, and I believe the win-win paradigm is partially responsible. So what if the negotiator settled for offering a 27 percent volume discount, while his bosses were hoping he'd only have to offer 24. He tried, and it's only a 3 percent difference, and it was win-win, so break out the bubbly. No one has any idea how much, if any, volume discount *should* have been offered and would have been accepted. Or change the perspective: The *buyer* was hoping to get a 27 percent discount but only got 24, and under win-win who knows how much she could have gotten with better negotiating? So break out the bubbly on the other side of the table.

My book introduces a *system*. With it, you *do* know how much discount should have been offered, and you do *not* offer one dime more. With my system, you focus on goals and behavior you can control and ignore results you cannot control. The system is pretty simple to understand, I believe, in its basics, but it does take strict discipline and a great deal of practice to employ successfully, whether you're negotiating the price of a Pokémon card, a new house, or a multimillion-dollar deal for, or with, a multinational. This discipline and practice have changed the lives of my clients—not only because they're bringing home a lot more money than in the past, but in the broader context of a life lived with boss, coworkers, teammates, spouse, children, friends. No matter your walk in life, if you sat down and calculated the number of negotiations you handle in a busy week, the answer would astound you. I did this once for myself and got up to one hundred before deciding that enough was enough. Your answer will be in the same range because, if your family is anything like mine was some years ago, which restaurant to go to with the kids is one negotiation, which table you take is a second one, what dishes they order is yet a third, and what they actually eat is yet a fourth. You get the picture. In New York City, which route the cabby takes from La Guardia to midtown Manhattan is a negotiation. What time you meet with your negotiating adversaries at the hotel may well be a negotiation. The list is endless, and the principles and system I introduce in this book apply to *all* of them.

The content of this book is contrarian, but the structure couldn't be more straightforward: fourteen chapters that introduce, one by one, the principles and practices of my system. They progress from the more general principles that are really about preparing *yourself* for negotiation—neediness, being *not* okay—to principles that are still about preparing yourself, but also take you into the realm of actual negotiations. These chapters will also be new to you, even when dealing with tried-and-true business ideas like mission and purpose, which, in my system, is completely different from any M&P statement you've ever prepared. The last chapters then take us into the nitty-gritty practices we'll use to negotiate actual deals. You will learn how to rigorously structure the negotiating process from A to Z with agendas and budgets and other good things—none of them being the usual practices of the business world.

A Bio and a Guarantee

This system first began to take shape in the air force, then during my career as a commercial pilot, and then in the business arena as I made the transition to negotiating coach. I am not a consultant. I'm a *coach,* and there's a huge difference: Consultants are much less hands-on than coaches, and they take no responsibility for their work. There are hundreds—maybe thousands—of consultants who include negotiations as a featured service. There are very few coaches who do what I do, working with my clients on *every* aspect of the negotiation.

For the past dozen years, since I founded the Negotiator Coaching Series in the Bay Area, and then Camptraining, I have trained and coached negotiation teams here and abroad, on every continent. I hold Negotiator Coach Symposiums every year in major venues across the continent. Harvard University, Ohio State University, and the University of San Francisco have sent participants to my lectures and symposiums. *Inc.* magazine has featured me in its annual Growing the Company conference. All in all, I've introduced my ideas and my system to about fifteen thousand individuals. I've worked with about 150 corporations on literally thousands of negotiations. In the last decade,

men and women in many different fields have used my system to
negotiate transactions worth more than $4 billion.

I've coached individuals and teams at such companies as
Motorola, Texas Instruments, Merrill Lynch, IBM, and Prudential Insurance. I also work with many medium-sized and small
companies. At any given time I'm working with about thirty
companies, conducting seminars and/or one-to-one coaching
with, on average, about 130 individuals in each company. I'm
involved in about 750 negotiations a year. I also coach some individual proprietors. And then there's the interactive website,
Camptraining.com.

I'm not claiming that this book will accomplish for the reader
what I accomplish with my workshops and hands-on and website coaching, because I work with my clients for hours, days,
weeks, months, years, and decades, in certain instances. I'm in-
clined to give credence to the theories of learning that suggest
we humans need about eight hundred hours to truly master a
complex concept and the habits necessary for its application. But
I have no doubt this book alone will be a revelation to readers,
just as the material in its more hands-on form is a revelation to
my clients. Think of me as a patient, supportive, enthusiastic
coach in absentia, or at a distance. Reading this book will not
necessarily prepare you for negotiating a $2 million deal with
Humongous, Inc., whose negotiators may be the most tenacious
of them all, but if you apply the principles I introduce here and
if you develop the proper habits, you will be closer to this goal
than you ever imagined.

Obviously, there are thousands of articles, books, college
courses, and websites dealing with the art and the science of negotiating. Plenty of good deals were signed in this world before
I showed up on the scene, and plenty have been accomplished by

negotiators who have never heard of me. But many, many bad ones have also been signed. This is my promise to the reader: You might pull off a successful negotiation—or at least obtain a serendipitous result—without the Camp System, but you will negotiate many more good deals *with* this system, and you will not get bogged down or suckered into a single bad negotiation *with* this system.

No one hires, or should hire, a negotiating trainer or coach based on an advertisement. Every new client I have is a referral from another client. In the early days of my work as a coach I offered every new client a written guarantee. If it were possible to publish a book with the same guarantee, I'd do so without qualms. If you work hard to understand and put to good use the principles and practices revealed in this short book, you *will* become an immeasurably better negotiator. That's a fact.

Whether we like it or not, it really is a jungle out there in the world of business, and it's crawling with predators. In my work I often use the image "dance with the tiger," because the tiger is viewed or even worshiped around the world as the ultimate predator. To dance well—to negotiate well—we must hear the music, we must *feel* the music, we must be tuned in to our partner—our "adversary"—at all times, we must follow carefully established steps with discipline. This book provides such a discipline and such a system. This is not a lot of theory that was dreamed up in an ivory tower and looks pretty good on paper but doesn't pass the smell test. My system was developed in the real world of business and is used with tremendous success in this real world every day. I've spent a good deal of time in the ivory tower, reading about the great decision makers, but I've never lived or worked there.

This is nuts-and-bolts material that you will *immediately* be able to apply in your business negotiations as well as in all other aspects of your life. You will learn how to lay out a negotiation on paper and control it step-by-step, how to react effectively to *anything* that happens at the negotiating table, how never to be caught flat-footed, even how to walk away with a smile, if need be. You will close this book feeling, "I can do this. What's more, I already have a pretty good idea *how* to do this."

1

Your Greatest Weakness in Negotiation

The Dangers of Neediness

WHY ARE THE tiger's eyes set in the front of the head, facing forward? Because the animal is a *predator* always on the lookout for prey. Why are our own eyes also set in the front of the head, facing forward? Because we are predators as well. Watching children in a playground is delightful, but it is also cautionary, as every parent knows, because we see the king-of-the-hill, one-upmanship, bullying, competitive instincts emerge at a very early age. These instincts last a lifetime, as anyone who has spent much time in a nursing home knows. They accompany some of us right to the grave.

This is a harsh truth with which to begin the first chapter of this book, but it's a vitally necessary point. Like all predators, we humans often take advantage of the fear-racked, the distressed, the vulnerable, the *needy*. We're capable of wonderful altruism as

well, but we don't find too much altruism in the business and
negotiation world, despite all the sweet talk of some cagey win-
win negotiators. In a negotiation, "dog-eat-dog" may not do
justice to the hidden ferocity. In your life as a negotiator, even in
your life as a private citizen of the world, you are dealing with
some serious predators who are looking for the slightest sign of
distress and neediness.

It is absolutely imperative that you as a negotiator understand
the importance of this point. You do NOT need this deal, because to be needy is to lose control and make bad decisions.

How vulnerable are you to predators when you lose control?
Very vulnerable. I'll illustrate the point with the movie *To Walk
with Lions,* starring Richard Harris and set in East Africa, naturally enough, where the character played by Harris has many
"friends" among the animals, including a certain lion. One day
Harris slips and falls on a hillside—and the lion is on him in a
flash! Harris manages to fire his gun and scare the lion away, but
he doesn't shoot him, because he has always known and never
forgotten that the lion is a predator, first and foremost, and will
behave like a predator when given the opportunity and sensing
weakness. Every animal trainer knows the same thing: with a
predator, it's all about power.

Many negotiators are the same way. Many *win-win* negotiators
are the same way. When I cover this subject in workshops and
seminars, some people seem to think that I'm exaggerating
about this neediness business. I am not. In fact, if I polled my
clients over the past years to name the one idea of my system
that had the greatest and *most immediately beneficial impact* on their
negotiating work, I'm pretty sure that a plurality, maybe even a
significant majority, would identify this simple warning about
neediness. With experience they have learned that neediness can

have—*will* have—a dramatic, always *negative* effect on their behavior. You must overcome any neediness at the negotiating table.

Neediness Comes in Many Varieties

Perhaps the category of negotiation in which this neediness dynamic is most powerful and dangerous is the straight retail sales negotiation, in which the golden rule of business is the implicit understanding of both sides: "The one with the gold rules."

In Western culture, we see ourselves as buyers, don't we? We proudly buy and consume as much as we can. The salesperson, on the other hand, has a problem with his or her self-image. The very term "sales" is being replaced in many fields by "business development," because the image of the salesperson is that of the huckster on the street, almost. More important, the salesperson is definitely the *dependent* party in the negotiation. He or she must be prepared to give, to compromise, while the buyer takes everything he or she can get. After all, the buyer can go elsewhere, in most cases, but the poor seller *needs* this deal. The self-image of the individual in the selling role traps him or her in a neediness mode and often leads to bad deals.

Tough negotiators are experts at recognizing this neediness in their adversaries, and expert in *creating* it as well. Negotiators with giant corporations, in particular, will heighten the expectations of their supplier adversaries, painting rosy, exaggerated scenarios for mega-orders, joint ventures, global alliances, all for the purpose of building neediness on the part of their adversary for this once-in-a-lifetime, career-making deal. Then, when the neediness is well established, they lower the boom with changes, exceptions, and a lot more—demands for concessions, all of them. Throughout this book we'll see in ugly detail how this works.

Sometimes, however, the buyer, not the seller, finds himself in the potentially needy position. A classic example from history is the Lewis and Clark expedition. When these intrepid explorers really *needed* fresh horses, the Native Americans somehow knew this. If the local residents were negotiating to sell less valuable and necessary goods, they came to quick agreements, but when they were selling vitally needed horses to the explorers, they pitched their teepees and settled in for the long haul. They were instinctively tough negotiators. (The journals of Lewis and Clark are excellent reading for any negotiator, because these two great Americans encountered dozens of unusual negotiating situations.)

Sometimes Lewis and Clark *were* needy, plain and simple. Sometimes they really were desperate for horses and other supplies. Today, in the twenty-first century, we're not needy. We're just not, but we nevertheless still hear people say, "I *need* this jacket." Or "I *need* this car." Or "I *need* to make this call." Or "I *need* this job." Or "I *need* to talk to you." Or "I *need* this deal." We use the word "need" much too casually. The only things we truly *need* are the basics of physical survival—air, water, food, clothing, shelter—and everyone reading this book already has these. We also need the basics of intellectual and emotional well-being—love, family, friendship, satisfying work, hobbies, faith— each reader has his or her own list here. But it's a *short* list, and it does not—or should not—include the $500 jacket or the $100,000 car, because there are other jackets and cars. It should not include this particular job or sale or deal, because there are other jobs and sales and deals.

Nevertheless, neediness is everywhere. Let me tell you the

most instructive experience on this subject I've had in my own life. The time is 0-dark-30 hours (military lingo for early A.M.) on a cold, damp, foggy January morning in West Texas. This is the first morning on the flight line for my group of fighter pilot trainees. The room is full of young men, all second lieutenants, dressed in new green flight suits and black high-top boots, waiting for the flight commander. In walks Major Dave Miller, slightly gray at the temples, the perfect specimen of a fighter pilot, a veteran of the Red River Valley in Vietnam, site of some of the most intense aerial combat in history. "Atten-hut!" We jump to our feet and stand ramrod straight.

In a deep, confident voice he commands "Seats!" You never saw men sit down as quickly as this group did. Immediately he says, "Lieutenant Camp." I'm startled but gather my wits as best as I can, leap back up to attention, and answer, "Sir, yes sir!" Dave Miller says, "You have just taken off, you are three hundred feet above the ground and climbing. Instantly, everything goes quiet and you feel like someone is putting on the brakes. Your airspeed is at two hundred fifty knots and slowing. You suddenly realize both engines have quit. What are you going to do?"

My mind goes blank and my heart goes into orbit. It seems like forever, but then I hear myself say, "Well, sir, which runway am I on?" And believe it or not, I proceeded to *debate* this man, a seasoned veteran, my teacher, about how I should have handled that hypothetical situation. The correct answer to Miller's question was eject. *Eject?* He must be out of his mind. I'd never ejected in my life—never even considered it during my prior training. And on that morning I never considered that Miller was trying to save my life, while I was trying to show off by arguing that I could make it to a certain runway.

There's another word for all that early chutzpah and ego on

my part: neediness, plain and simple. In that "negotiation" with my instructor, I needed to be a top gun, to know it all, to be right. Sometimes neediness is blatant and easy to spot, as in that flying story, but more often it is subtle and insidious. The trained negotiator sees neediness of all sorts all the time, in big ways and in little ways. It is so easy to slip into such a state, often without even being aware of it.

Think about something as simple as a greeting.

"Hi, I'm Frank Jones."
"Hello, Mr. Jones."

Such subtle subservience puts you at an immediate disadvantage. You have conceded that Frank Jones is top gun in this room, and he knows it. You're ripe for the picking. So call him Frank instead.

Consider this appeal for an appointment:

"Mr. Smith, this is Bob Jones. I'm with First Advantage Venture Fund, and I want to see if I could get ten minutes on your calendar so I can show you how we can work with you in the future."

Remember, new companies aren't the only parties who can be needy. Some start-ups are well funded and choosy regarding any venture capitalist they may bring in. The investors can also get into the needy mode, just as Bob Jones did while more or less *begging* for this appointment. Bob should have said:

"Bill, my name is Bob Jones. I'm not quite sure that we as a venture fund fit where you're going. I just don't know. What I'd like to do is meet with you so we can see where you're going and you can look at where we're going at First Advantage and see if there's a fit. When's the best time on your calendar?"

"No Talking"

Talking can be an overt showing of need. This is why "No Talking" is one of my rules—an exaggeration, of course, but I make it a rule to make the point: Talking and showing need go hand in hand. One of my best students started out with an insatiable desire to make sure his voice was heard. This guy was bright and always wanted people to know that he was as informed and on top of things as anyone in the room. He needed to feel important. *Okay,* thought his shrewder adversaries, *we'll be happy to let you feel important as we skin you alive.* This is a common issue that hard-driving, alpha-male types have to deal with daily: They want to know it all, or, short of that, they want to be seen to know it all. The adrenaline kicks in, the neediness becomes a biochemical fact, then the neediness becomes a biochemical addiction. It's true.

One of the most effective life insurance salesmen I ever saw was a man in a wheelchair who could not speak. He used a marker and a board to communicate, patiently writing out his questions. I would not wish this man's disability on anyone, but his only means of asking questions was a terrific advantage in his profession, as he was the first to acknowledge, because it's hard to be needy while sitting in a wheelchair calmly writing out questions by hand. (His most effective question, by the way: "If we lose you, where will your family live?")

How many people do you know who won't let you get a word in edgewise? By being overbearing, these people are actually betraying neediness. I've even heard an overbearing, needy outgoing message on an answering machine. Normal is "Hi, this is ————. Please leave your message at the beep." Instead, this individual greeted the caller with a detailed message regarding her schedule for the hour, the day, the week. And I think we can imagine what kind of messages this person left on other people's answering machines: long ones! She needed to make sure you understood how busy she was, how competent she must be, how lucky you would be if she could spare you the time of day. But it's all counterproductive. It's just annoying.

Now think for a moment about "cold calls" and "warm calls," because they're the ultimate lesson on this subject. Just thinking about cold calls gives the average businessperson chills. It's tough, no doubt about it, and a lot of fine people just won't do it. Cold calling is the worst way to do business, we all know that. But I say it's also a great way, because it's a great training ground, and it can be surprisingly effective *because your neediness is under control.* You have no great expectations, that's for sure, and your discipline is keen. You start off by saying something like:

> *"Well, Mary, I have no idea whether what we do has any relevance for your business. I just don't know, maybe it doesn't. If not, just tell me and I'll be on my way, but if whoever handles your market research . . ."*

And off you go—or not. It doesn't matter. Your neediness is under control.

A cold call is just another negotiation—no more and no less—and by the end of this book you'll understand how to handle a cold call according to the same rules and habits as you would handle any other negotiation.

The same holds for a warm call:

> *"Hey, Tom, this is Bill. Man, do I have a hot one for you. I told them all about you, what you do. They're on the tee. They're ready. All you gotta do is call and then collect. You owe me one, buddy."*

Oh yeah? Tom's blood is racing, but he might be better off with a cold call than with a reference like that one. If he's not careful, he'll lose discipline, start thinking about the payday, get excited, become needy. That's when defeat may be snatched from the jaws of victory. Do yourself a favor: treat every warm call as though it's the coldest one you ever made.

When emotions run hot and heavy in negotiations, the high-pitched voice is a sure sign of need. The rushed delivery is another sure sign. While needy negotiators raise their voices, negotiators under control lower their voices. So lower your voice in times of inner turmoil. Slow down.

The Third World bazaar offers classic lessons on neediness, as I learned myself while Christmas shopping in Saigon in 1967, holding about $100 with which to buy presents for my whole family. My grandparents were very special to me, and I thought about them when I found in the same shop two beautiful pieces of lacquerware and a small boat carved from a water buffalo horn. Mama-san said she wanted 1,000 piastres apiece—about $10, or $30 total. I wanted all three in the worst way, but this was way too much money, and I said so. I was too young and naive to be employing any negotiating strategy, and I didn't want to be the proverbial ugly American, but I couldn't buy them. As I started to leave, Mama-san chased after me and said she'd sell them for 800 piastres each. I said no, it's still too much. I shopped elsewhere, bought some nice things and some trinkets, but I still had nothing for my grandparents as I was walking past the little shop with the lacquerware and the carved boat. When Mama-san saw me with the packages she grabbed me and said, "Oh, you number one GI, you beaucoup shop." She urged me back inside, where she offered to part with each of the three items for 500 piastres apiece, but this was still too much. "No," I said. "I'll give you four hundred, that's all I have." She said, "Okay, GI, I sell you for four hundred."

I wasn't needy. She was. But if she had been a Camp-trained negotiator, she'd have asked me (setting aside the language problem), "Who are these for?" When I answered she would have whistled and said, "Why would you want to spend so much money on them? A lot of money for grandparents." She would have shown no need while building *my* need. She'd have laid a guilt trip on me—*Money's not a factor when it comes to my grandparents!*—and I'd have paid 1,000 piastres, or darned close to it, because I really loved my grandparents.

Don't Worry About Rejection

Fear of rejection is a sign of neediness—specifically, the need to be liked. It is imperative for the negotiator to understand just what rejection is, and who can reject you and who cannot. Here's the key point: Your adversaries in a negotiation *cannot* reject you. There's nothing you need from them, so how can they reject you? It's impossible. The parent can reject the child, because the child certainly needs the parent. The spouse can reject the spouse. The teacher can even reject the student in the early grades, when the boy or girl truly does need this teacher. But can your adversary in a negotiation really reject you? They don't have any such power. Never, *never* allow them to believe that they do.

The serious negotiator understands that he or she cannot go out into the world spending emotional energy in the effort to be liked, to be smart, to be important. This negotiator wants to be recognized as being effective and businesslike, that's all. She spends her energy on the task of business. She has no need for the rest of it. But how often we fall into this particular neediness trap. In labor-management relationships, a key tactic of management is to find union members who want a boost to the ego and can therefore be made to feel needy. Such members can be manipulated until they are double agents for management, in effect, passing on contrived information, telling their own union members, "Our committee is getting us killed. I've got buddies in management. That's what they tell me. They might shut this plant down if we keep on like this."

I speak both from personal experience of many years ago— that labor-management dispute—and from my coaching experience, as I've seen negotiating team members undermine their own team in a host of ways. They leak valuable information, bring back false information, break their team's resolve, urge unnecessary compromises—all because their neediness to be smart, to be liked, to be important, is turned against them by the clever adversary. Off the top, I could name a dozen well-paid management professionals for Fortune 500 companies who were, in effect, working for their adversaries in big-time negotiations. I know because these adversaries were my clients. I can name an almost-at-the-top executive whose neediness for a deal to use as a stepping-stone to the chairmanship made him agree to a totally unnecessary compromise. The eventual deal camouflaged that compromise, but that's what it was. I know because the beneficiary of that ridiculous compromise was my client.

A few years ago, I took on a corporate client who had just lost a large deal with a multinational *after* my new client had compromised in every way imaginable. They had the best technology to start with, and on top of that they offered the best price, the best terms, the best delivery dates, the best service, the best everything. If they could compromise on any element of the negotiation, they did. They even tossed in a free piece of very expensive equipment, no strings attached. But the multinational walked away from this steal of a deal. Why? We finally found out that their CEO was wary precisely because the company that was now my client had compromised *too much*. Something must be wrong, he thought, for a company to show so much need. That cannot be a competent, trustworthy company. They'll never be able to deliver. And that CEO was right. My new client would never have been able to make good on the commitments negotiated in that deal.

Wanting Is Fine, Needing Is Not

The next time you watch one of the predator-prey nature shows on public television or one of the wildlife channels, watch the chase scenes carefully. There are always one or two in which the lion or the cheetah is not successful, and each time the scenario is the same: The predator gets closer to the prey . . . closer . . . closer, then slips back slightly—and *immediately* gives up. On the spot. When the distance to the prey begins to widen, the hunter quits. She (the females do most of the hunting) will never waste energy on a losing cause. She saunters off, because it doesn't matter. There are other wildebeests, other gazelles. Likewise, the trained negotiator has no needs, because it just doesn't matter. There are other deals. Turn the page on this one. Let it go.

I mentioned in the introduction one of my ironclad rules: "No Closing." The context was a discussion of the dangers of win-win, and how win-win implicitly urges you to focus on what you cannot control—the end—while losing sight of what you can control—the means. Now I'll add the point that urgent closing betrays neediness on your own part. You *need* to close.

No, you don't. But maybe your adversary does.

The personal experience of every single reader of this book reveals the dangers of the trick closing. When someone has tried to close on you too quickly—and someone has, in one context or another, unless you're still a babe in arms—you instinctively reacted in the negative. Nothing, but nothing, will blow a negotiation faster than such a rush to judgment. Why? You had a vision of neediness, which makes anyone feel uncomfortable emotionally, and which also serves as a warning to look closer at this deal.

More bad deals are signed and more sales are lost because of neediness than because of any other single factor. If there's any need in this negotiation it has to be your adversary's, not yours. You will never achieve the level of success of which you're capable until you understand and *live* this concept. We negotiators—we humans—show our neediness in many, many ways. To recognize your own varieties, all you really have to do is stop and think about what you're doing and what the underlying motivation is. No one knows better than you when your neediness is showing its true colors. When you stop to consider, it's amazing how much in our lives that we get so worked up over doesn't matter, not really.

As a negotiator aspiring to excellence, you must, at all costs, avoid showing need. In order to avoid showing need, you must never *feel* it. You do *not* need this deal. But what happens if we simply substitute the word and the emotion "want" for "need"? The dynamics change. What picture comes to mind when you read the words "I want"? I see a bright red Porsche convertible, with a black top and interior. What is your picture? As good negotiators, the word "want" means something we work for, strive for, plan for, but it is never confused with "need." Sure I *want* this global alliance with Humongous, Inc., but I don't *need* it. I want the car, but I don't need it. I want the house, but I don't need it. It will be their loss, not mine, if any of these deals falls through. Either way, I'll sleep tonight and I'll eat tomorrow.

Camp-trained negotiators never show need, only want. "Need" is death, "want" is life. Believe me, this different attitude will be instantly perceived by the folks on the other side of the table. Confidence and trust go up across the board. Control and discipline go up for you.

I hope I haven't sounded like a broken record (or should I bring myself up to date and say CD?) in this chapter, but I can't say this too often: Overcome all need.

2

The Columbo Effect
The Secret of Being "Not Okay"

REMEMBER THE OLD TV series *Columbo*? Or perhaps you watch the reruns every night. As a homicide detective in Los Angeles, Columbo wore the raggedy trench coat, drove the beat-up old Peugeot, told heartwarming stories about his wife and his dog—a sad-looking basset hound, I believe, definitely not a silky-sleek golden retriever—and he had the habit of forgetting to ask a key question in every interview and interrogation. He'd have to ring the doorbell again, apologize, and ask that final question. He always presented himself to his adversaries as a little less competent than they were, a little less perfect—or, usually, a lot less perfect. He could get people to talk to him because he made them feel superior and therefore comfortable. In the lingo made famous by the book *I'm Okay, You're Okay*, he seduced them into feeling okay.

To be okay is to feel comfortable and therefore safe. That's the simplest way to define the word as it's used in pop psychology. From the moment of birth, all of us, as members of the human race, struggle to feel comfortable and safe. As babies and toddlers, we need—we demand!—the unconditional love of our parents that is the *only* source of our well-being. As young children, our demands in this regard increase. We want to be recognized. We wanted to be heard. We want to be liked. We want to be right. Or should I say we *need* all this? I'm afraid so. And this *need* to feel okay follows us right through adolescence and into adulthood as we struggle for victory, achievement, success. When we're called upon to show ourselves, do we expose our weakness? Never. We expose our strength. Maybe our strength is our knowledge, or physical beauty, or charming personality. Maybe we are cunning and fearless, or quick of wit. Whatever our strength, that is what we build on. That is what we show the world. This is what we *need* to show the world.

Likewise, we compare ourselves to others in order to see how we stack up. Are we a little ahead or a little behind? When we are with people we think we are ahead of, or at least equal to, we feel comfortable. Conversation comes easily and questions seem to have no risk. We feel okay. But in the presence of people to whom we feel inferior, whether culturally, socially, or intellectually, we feel unokay and can become defensive, or aggressive, or resentful, or a lot of other emotions. When someone looks perfect while we need a haircut, how do we feel? Exactly. A little uneasy, a little unokay. Conversation may be difficult, questions seem full of risk, we fear we will look silly or even stupid.

Turning the situation around, have you noticed how we humans tend to feel okay when we see someone *not* okay? We feel comfortable when we see someone who doesn't quite measure up in some way. Soap opera fans watch the shows because the lives of the characters in those stories are even more messed up than the viewers' own lives. We revel in the trials and tribulations of the rich and famous because now the tables are turned: A lot of good their fame and fortune has brought them! Suddenly we're more okay than the movie star in the $2,000-a-day rehab center. This is not our most attractive feature, perhaps, but there it is. Long ago the Germans gave this feeling the name *Schadenfreude*.

I don't guess anyone really argues these points about okayness. They're pretty self-evident. But my next statement is far from self-evident. At first blush, in fact, it will sound crazy to many readers (as it has to many of my clients), but here goes: The wise negotiator knows that only one person in a negotiation can feel okay, and that person is the *adversary*.

Some new clients are not just baffled by this lesson, but positively antagonistic. The lesson is correct, however, and extraordinarily effective as a tool in a negotiation. By letting your adversary be a little more okay, you start to bring down barriers. By allowing him to feel in control, you, like Columbo, are actually in control. The detective's sad-sack behavior was calculated. His adversary doesn't know this, but we viewers do. We also understand *why* he acts this way. We understand the psychology: Columbo solved every crime by allowing his adversaries to feel more okay.

I'll cite a few parallel examples from history. Ronald Reagan, intentionally or unintentionally, was a master at appearing less than okay at press conferences. He would stammer around and laugh at himself before he answered a question, and then his answer might not have been much of one at all. But he was effective, wasn't he, in the end? Winston Churchill was an unprepossessing butterball, FDR a crippled man in a wheelchair, Abraham Lincoln one of the less attractive men around, but these three leaders did well enough, in the end. And one final example: what did General Norman Schwarzkopf do when he opened the negotiation with King Fahd of Saudi Arabia to base American troops and airplanes on Saudi soil as we moved toward war with Iraq in 1990? The four-star general dropped to one knee. (Not out of *neediness,* note, but out of unokayness. Neediness is an internal state, unokayness a public presentation.)

Surely you've noticed how every effective keynote and after-dinner speaker tells a self-deprecating story in the first few minutes of his performance. His first implicit message to the audience: You may be paying me ten grand to stand up here, and my suit may be more expensive than yours, but I'm no better than you, I'm just folks. And this is not gamesmanship. This is *honesty,* because, in the final analysis, everyone on this planet is just folks, one of the gang—a big gang, to be sure, but just a gang. We're all in this boat together. We're all human. We've all made a mistake today and we'll make another one tomorrow, very possibly a whopper. People who pretend otherwise fool no one but themselves (if they really fool themselves).

As negotiators, we must take the same approach. If you can emulate Columbo's *unokayness* to even a small degree, in your own way, you will exponentially increase your negotiating success.

In his profound essay "On Compensation," Ralph Waldo Emerson wrote, "Our greatest strength is our greatest weakness." How true. We tend to overplay our hand, so to speak, but as negotiators we must control this instinct while letting it blossom in our adversary. If he likes to show off his glibness, let him. If he can't resist the opportunity to play to his charm, let him. If he likes to demonstrate his extraordinary grasp of the finest points of federal maritime law, let him. The trained negotiator is more than happy to let the adversary show off in almost any way he wants to, because that adversary's greatest strength will eventually become his greatest weakness.

Some years back I worked with a company I'll call Network, Inc., that was on the brink of bankruptcy. If this company had continued to ship its product at the contracted price with its primary customer, it would have gone out of business because it was losing $100,000 with every machine it shipped. Renegotiation was called for. Either that or bankruptcy. However, no one in the organization thought they should reopen the negotiation. They thought this move would look "unprofessional." They said, "We're going to look like fools." The president balked as well, until I finally got his attention by asking, "How long do you want to continue to tape a $100,000 check to the side of each machine?"

When the president of Network called his adversary to broach the subject, he said, in just about so many words, "You have done such a great job negotiating, and we are so incompetent and so weak in negotiating, that we have been a poor supplier. We have put you in a terrible position, and we apologize for that. We take responsibility for our ineptness in negotiation." This was the truth, and it needed to be said, but it was also effective in the way of Columbo. This helped to disarm the adversary. Nor was it unprofessional to make such an admission. That adversary is now my client's biggest customer.

Another one of my corporate clients today does business in a field with a lot of negotiators trained in PICOS or one of the other supply systems management methodologies. These are really tough professionals, notorious within the industry.

They've called my negotiators names and accused them of un-professional behavior, real in-your-face tactics. (Sometimes these fellows will be your best friend and wine and dine you, then turn on a dime and intimidate you with bluster.) Do my clients get needy? Do they get defensive and then aggressive and fight back against this behavior? No. They listen calmly, they take notes, they make a concerted effort to be not okay, and then they ask quietly, "What would you like us to do?"

So Effective It's Scary

I am *not* suggesting that you appear unprofessional. I'm asking you not to be afraid of candor and honesty, not to be afraid of not being totally okay, of being less than perfect. Do you enjoy being around the perfect person? I don't. People want to deal with a regular person. In a negotiation, being less okay is just showing a foible now and then. Struggle a little. Borrow a pen or paper to take notes. Search for the right words to ask questions. Letting people help you is an excellent way to help them feel more okay. It also says to your adversary, "What you see is what you get."

New clients think I must be kidding when I even suggest they leave their briefcase or business cards at home for the first meeting, and maybe you just won't do it, but I'm here to tell you that this gambit or something similar can be so powerful it's scary. I once coached a woman who sold office equipment to Silicon Valley start-ups. In one negotiation in which a $35,000 commission was at stake, I finally convinced her to drop her purse onto the floor. Only thing was, when the purse hit the floor it fell open and the contents spilled everywhere. A real mess. The guy she was negotiating with hurried around the desk and got down on his knees to help my client gather everything up. As she was expressing her embarrassment, he was saying, "Hey, forget it. You've got the deal."

Again, some might call this gamesmanship, but I disagree. My client didn't get the deal because she dropped her purse. She got the deal because the purse episode broke through the final barrier in the negotiation, allowing decisions to flow freely. This is not trivial gamesmanship. This is honesty, the honesty of unokayness that breaks down barriers.

The tougher the negotiation, the more critical it is to understand that if someone in this room has to be unokay, it will be you and not your adversary. When your adversary feels unokay, the barriers go up much faster than you can break them down. But unokayness on your part breaks down barriers—like magic, often.

This behavior is all easier said than done, I realize, because from the day we're born we're fighting for our okayness, and then we're almost *trained* to fight for it. And of course we see pictures of the titans of industry—maybe the CEO of the very company we work for—dressed to the nines as they savor their power breakfasts, power lunches, power dinners, power aperitifs, and power cigars. These guys (they are mostly guys, let's face it) are okay beyond belief. Their lives are what we're supposed to want and *need*. And here I am suggesting that you get to the top by presenting yourself as less okay!

In the context of a negotiation, yes I am. I'm not saying you show up with a stain on your shirt or blouse. Just a little something that's less than perfect to inject a little humanity, a little vulnerability, a little unokayness. The truly skillful, successful negotiator gets his or her strokes at home. (If you're fortunate, you're like former president Jerry Ford or former First Ladies

Barbara Bush and the late Jackie O., all of whom were famous for their instinctive ability to make people around them and people watching on television feel okay. But if you're like . . . well, never mind, you'll have to work a little harder. Some people just seem to have the unfortunate knack of making others feel un-okay.)

If you have any doubts about the wisdom of the advice in this chapter, it couldn't be easier to check out. The next time you find yourself in a situation in which your "adversary" is maybe just a little standoffish or doubtful, try being a little less okay. Pretend your pen has run out of ink and ask to borrow one for a moment. Or search your pocket for your notepad and come up short and ask to borrow a slip of paper. Or pretend your Palm Pilot has run out of power—again. And then try to tell me you don't notice an immediate, beneficial difference in the atmosphere of this "negotiation."

3

Start with No

How Decisions Move
Negotiations Forward

WHEN YOU BECOME excited or nervous, where in your body do you feel it first? Where do you get butterflies before a speech or public performance of any kind? When was the last time you heard someone say, "He just doesn't have the stomach for it"? Do you remember one important time when you said to someone, "My gut tells me I shouldn't do this"? Yes, probably. In Japan, where negotiation is revered almost as a cultural art form, it is said that we should make all of our decisions with the stomach—*hara*—never with the head or with the heart. I absolutely agree that this is where decisions *start*. This is the way we *do* make decisions, whether we like the idea or not.

In a negotiation, decisions are 100 percent emotional. Yes, 100 percent. Research psychologists have proved this beyond any doubt. Sometimes we use the term "negotiation science," but the "science" part is knowing that decisions themselves are all emotion. In a Camp negotiation, it is *always* gut-check time, because this is where the real negotiation is being played out.

When was the last time you presented some facts and figures that made perfect sense in your own head and should have made perfect sense in your adversary's head, but he still couldn't agree with you? Couldn't even see what you were talking about? I'm sure it's happened, because facts do not win negotiations. Facts come later, because they mean nothing to the stomach. Or consider the smoking habit. You probably know a smoker who claims he can quit anytime he "decides" to do so. When does he quit? Sadly, in many cases, only after he has had to have quadruple bypass heart surgery—and not always then, unbelievably. If facts aren't able to convince most smokers to break the habit that is literally killing them, it's small wonder that facts do not win negotiations, either. The head is too confused, or too rigid, but mainly it's just out of the loop. The real decisions are being made somewhere else. Our so-called rational mind kicks in only *after* we've made the decision, in order to justify it after the fact.

When we watch ourselves and other people carefully, we can actually see the transition from the emotional state—the *hara*—to the intellectual state—the head. Every day, every hour, even every minute, under some circumstances, we flip back and forth between the emotional and the so-called rational. Our emotions rage all over the scale before we make a decision, and then we set about rationalizing it. Successful negotiation requires the complete understanding and application of this dynamic of decision making.

But wait a minute. Don't these paragraphs contradict the claim in the introduction that my system is decision based, *not* emotion based? How can this be, if all negotiations are emotional? Negotiations and even decision making do *begin* with emotions. Emotions are rampant, they are at the root of our initial decisions, they are unreliable, they are even destructive, but these emotions do *not* have to be the final word. My system sees emotions for what they are and works with them, not against them. My system teaches us how to progress *from* emotions, which never produce deals that stick, to *decisions* that do produce deals that stick.

Negotiations are indeed rooted in emotions, and all too often never get beyond them. Your job as a negotiator is to see them clearly and overcome them with precise decision making. Your job is even to use them to your advantage with precise decision making. The subject of this chapter is the subtle relationship between emotion and decision making, and the ways in which you can capitalize on your understanding of this relationship.

Forget "Yes," Forget "Maybe"

I like to provoke new clients and folks in seminars and workshops by stating that the best "yes" in a negotiation is by way of "no." I tried to provoke you, the reader, with *Start with No* as my title, but the phrase is a lot more than a mere provocation. It's also the truth. The negotiation really does start with "no"—not with "maybe," definitely not with "yes," but with a firm, clear "no." In any negotiation, this is the key word I want to hear. Everything that precedes it is mere window dressing.

How can this be? Because "no" is a real decision that induces the party across the table into actually thinking about why they've just said "no." The responsibility of making a clear decision helps the adversary focus on the real issues of the negotiation. The adversary has to take responsibility for "no," so now everyone has something real to talk about. In fact, as we will soon see, the mere *invitation* for the other side to say "no" changes the dynamic of a negotiation in a very beneficial way. But the alternative answers—"maybe" and "yes"—aren't real decisions at all. They do nothing at all to stop the ebb and flow of emotions. They're just a frustrating waste of time. Let's see why.

With "maybe," neither party has any idea where things stand. If you say "maybe," you haven't said enough to elicit a useful response or information from the other side, because you haven't really said anything at all. You've muddied the waters, nothing more. Likewise, when you *hear* "maybe," your emotions are all over the place. Did he really mean "yes"? Are we almost there? Or is he just trying a last-minute ploy for concessions? Or did he really mean "No, this offer doesn't have a chance"? Or did he actually mean "maybe" because he doesn't even know what he wants? Well, who the heck has any idea? I could even suggest that "maybe" is more of an emotion than anything else. It definitely isn't a decision. It definitely does not engage the negotiator's rational mind. It definitely doesn't give either side anything to work with.

I cannot emphasize this point too strongly: "Maybe" is the kiss of death for a successful negotiation. If you can't quickly get past "maybe"—and it comes in infinite varieties, of course—start walking, because you're wasting your time (especially when dealing with the Japanese, who will drive the untrained negotiator crazy with "maybe").

Sometimes even "maybe" is too harsh sounding for the faint of heart who doesn't want to hurt our feelings and perhaps endanger the negotiation. Sometimes the adversary is so conditioned by the "getting to yes" ethos that she *starts out* with "yes." But a "yes" in the beginning is no better than a "maybe." It is not a decision, not really, because your adversary can't really mean "yes." If she did, everyone wouldn't be here *negotiating* in the first place.

More important, when our adversaries say "yes," we get excited, our adrenaline starts pumping, we start computing the commission and deciding between the Mercedes and the Beemer—and before we know it, we're . . . what? Needy. And the moment we're needy, we've lost control. We know in our head that this "yes" isn't real and final, but the emotion in our heart surges nevertheless. And then, hours or days or weeks later, when this "yes" is followed by the adversary's subtle "if," "but," "however," "when," or some other dangerous qualifier, we've lost our focus and become vulnerable to unnecessary compromise. The other side is suddenly in control. Offering an early "yes" is a real tiger trick. It traps us in his cage. Shrewd corporate negotiators use this trick all the time.

"Maybe" is worthless and "yes" is dangerous, so we're left with "no," a real decision. As I said, "no" gets the adversary across the table into a rational mode. Just *thinking* about saying "no" gets the adversary into the rational mode. Elucidation is required, and now you have real issues to discuss. Ross Perot's negotiator out in the desert should have been delighted, not disappointed, to hear the bedouin say "no" regarding the selected camel.

Let's consider a classic situation encountered by almost every smaller company that negotiates with multinationals. Specifically, a large multinational was negotiating with three different, much smaller companies for a special project, playing the competitors against one another, asking for one concession after another from one competitor after another, driving the price down, down, down. Finally, the company that had been the multinational's first choice—I'll call it Bonanza, Inc.—got tired of this whipsawing and decided to either change the dynamic or drop out of the negotiation. Their negotiators told the multinational that Bonanza could not and would not participate in any further reductions, so Bonanza probably was not the company for the project. In short, Bonanza said "no," which was an invitation for the multinational to say "no" in return.

Now the much bigger company faced a couple of tough issues. They might not be able to get the best company for the project, and the other companies might take the same stance as Bonanza. They could no longer play the three companies against one another. Because one company was willing to risk losing the deal rather than compromise further, the multinational's negotiators found themselves at a severe disadvantage. We can guess what happened next. That company began to disclose information to Bonanza, the very company that had told them "no," thereby giving Bonanza a great advantage. In the end, this is the company that got the project.

That's the power of "no." Now, what would have happened if the multinational had been Camp trained and said early on to Bonanza and the other two companies, "Feel free to say no. Turn us down at any point"? The negotiation would have proceeded much more quickly. Essential issues, not emotional ones, would have been on the table early. Neither side would have been in a guessing mode. Everyone would have known how everyone else saw the negotiation. Everyone could have been working on real problems. Time, money, and resources would have been saved.

That's the key idea here: "no" gets you past emotional issues and trivial issues to *essential* issues. We want decision-based negotiation, not the emotion-based waste of time known as win-win.

I mentioned that the use of the worthless "maybe" is an art form in Japan. Now here's a "no" story set in that esteemed country, one in which a new American-based client was stuck with a terrible distribution deal with a Japanese giant. This deal had been negotiated by my client's win-win team years before, and it was losing millions of dollars annually. Really, it was running the business into the ground, and everyone at the board level understood that the deal had to be renegotiated *now*, even though contractually it couldn't be challenged for another five losing years. However, and predictably, everyone who had negotiated the old agreement argued that the company would ruin its position in Japan and never recover when word spread that we wanted to renegotiate. You just can't operate that way in Japan, the old crowd warned. It's impossible. But the president of the company decided that the only thing impossible was continuing with the ridiculous deal signed by that incompetent team of win-win negotiators.

Eighteen months after the subject of renegotiation was first broached, the issue finally reached the highest level of the Japanese company, where the American team presented a new deal, all the while urging the Japanese to just say "no" if they felt they had to. Our agreement must change, my clients said, but tell us "no" if this new one doesn't work for you. Just say, "We can't do this." The Japanese sucked their teeth—literally—and talked among themselves for at least twenty minutes. They recessed. My clients waited calmly. Finally, the Japanese came back and said they'd accept the proposal we gave them. Period.

The invitation to say "no" crystallized their thinking. It got their attention. If they *had* said "no" in response to us, fine, we would have dug into the details of our offer and negotiated from that point. As it was, the invitation to say "no" led directly, inexorably, to a deal. And what about the dire prediction of a ruined business relationship with that Japanese distributor—ruined prospects in Japan, period? Hogwash. The two companies now have a mutually profitable—very profitable—relationship.

A few hundred miles west of Japan is Korea, where the businesspeople are also known as tenacious negotiators who always get their way. My client in this Korean story, a player in one of the high-tech industries, was negotiating with a Korean giant regarding extremely complicated and vital equipment. The giant was rightly convinced they needed this technology, but they insisted on a lot of it for free. This was a perfectly natural demand, because, as many readers know, a lot of American companies believe they have to give away technology and equipment in order to get a foot in the door of that society and economy. I'm not talking about a $200,000 piece of equipment, either. I'm talking about tens and hundreds of millions of dollars in factories and technology given away *for free*. How did American companies get the idea that they had to do this? Because the Koreans asked for it, and we all know how tough those Koreans are. To my knowledge, corporate America had never once said, "No, we don't think so, we believe in a fair profit for our business. Feel free to say no to us in return, but we're not giving you a good piece of our business for nothing. That's not a good practice for us and our investors."

Now, my client's sales force in Korea was Camp trained, and they understood that Camp-trained negotiators don't compromise for the fun of it and don't give away the store simply because someone *asks* for the store. But they assured their chiefs at headquarters on the mainland that the Camp System wouldn't work in Korea, because a generous sweetener is the way business works over there. We have to forget our training, they insisted, but the president of the company insisted otherwise. He didn't feel like giving anything away. He instructed his salespeople to negotiate full price for the machines. A daunting task, certainly, but the team returned to Korea and made its presentation, inviting the Koreans at every opportunity to say "no." Sure enough, the adversaries came unglued. *You can't do business like that here!* These protestations went on three days. Finally my clients said they would be leaving the following morning, and very politely gave the Koreans one last chance to say "no" and be done with it. But the Koreans didn't do that, and the team flew home without either a firm "no" or an order for machines.

Three days later the phone rang at company headquarters. The Koreans placed an order worth $30 million, complete with a purchase order number. They paid full price, because full price is a fair price for this state-of-the-art technology, and they had known this all along. But why not try to get something for nothing, they had figured—and who could blame them, because that tactic had been working for years and years against lackluster win-win negotiators from America.

Back now in the States with a different scenario: A client that builds expensive machinery was just about to ship the first order to a new customer when the customer called to say that they also needed a separate machine that worked in tandem with the main order. My client's salesman who was responsible for this deal wanted to consign the separate item on the spot and be a hero in the eyes of the new customer. But this item wasn't easily available, and his superiors with my client decided to say no, the equipment wasn't available, there was an eight-week delivery, they didn't know what they could do to help. That answer was transmitted on Friday night. On Saturday morning, my client called the customer again and said that they *could* juggle things around and deliver the other equipment, but at some risk to the bottom line, so could the customer help out here by taking two older machines and paying within the month? The customer accepted the new terms immediately. *Then,* on Monday, the customer called to say that *they* had turned up the separate equipment they needed, so they didn't need the favor after all. My client calmly said okay, but we did do a lot of juggling here on your behalf, we'd like you to buy the two old systems anyway. Say no if you want to, it'll be okay, no hard feelings, but we think the fair thing is for you to buy the two old systems.

The customer agreed.

The Power of "No"

Saying "no," *inviting* "no," *hearing* "no": these are all-powerful tools for *any* well-trained negotiator, including a high school kid I knew a few years ago, an athlete applying to colleges. Like all valuable high school recruits, he had been inundated with solicitation letters from programs all over the country. He had two big garbage bags full of letters he never even opened. (I guess computer programs spit out these invitations by the thousands.) To the coaches at the schools in which he was interested, this student sent his academic transcript along with a letter requesting that the recruiter please advise him if he was not academically qualified. That was a straightforward "tell me no" request. The player didn't want to waste his time with a school for which he was not qualified. Later in the negotiation (what else would you call it?), he followed up with a second request for certain coaches to tell him "no." To them he wrote, "Please tell me if you're not going to support my application through the admissions process. I'd appreciate knowing this now, because if you cannot support me, I'll move on to the other schools I'm interested in."

He didn't know precisely how much sway the coach had in the admissions process, he did know that the number of student-athletes was limited, and he knew that the admissions committee would not select these lucky kids without input from the coach. With the coach's stamp of approval, his chances would rise exponentially. A coach's commitment to supporting his application was as close to an assured acceptance as he could get. The easiest way to accomplish both these goals—finding out where he stood and getting the coach on his side—was to ask the coach to say "no."

Helped by his requests for "nos," he received a bunch of "yeses." I relate this college recruiting story to demonstrate that many situations that we might not think of as "negotiations" really are, and that "just say no" is an effective tool in *every single one of them.*

In the discussion on neediness in chapter 1, I suggested the cold caller begin the conversation: "Well, Mary, I have no idea whether what we do has any relevance for your business. I just don't know, maybe it doesn't. If not, just tell me and I'll be on my way, but if whoever handles your market research . . ." See how that statement invites the adversary to say "no"? Establishing this ground rule is just so critical in *all* negotiations. But when was the last time any of those phone companies or stockbrokers or bankers who call at dinnertime ever invited you to send him on his way? Would your temptation to slam down the phone have been slightly tempered if he had? "No!" you say. "I'd slam down the phone anyway." And maybe you would, but

I'm here to tell you that a good script that begins with a calm invitation to say no will generate about *three* good appointments for every *ten* calls, which is an unbelievable percentage, as I'm sure you'll agree.

I'm not just spouting off on this subject. I know what I'm talking about, because in the early days of my coaching career I built my first client base with cold calls as well as with referrals. I called people in insurance, real estate, advertising, stockbrokerage, and accounting, and said, "Pete, I'm not sure that anything I do fits with you. I don't know. So if this doesn't make any sense, just tell me and I'll get off the phone. Is that fair?" If Pete invited me to proceed—and he usually did—I then asked, "Who do you have in your corner, Pete, who can assure you that your income will increase through coaching?"

In those early days I worked with insurance companies and their sales staffs, and I could *guarantee* that after eighteen hours of training, a group of thirty salespeople would net ninety valid appointments with just two hours of calling apiece. That's an incredible return on investment of time, as anyone in that field knows.

Eight or nine years ago, my oldest son, Jimmy, had some time after he graduated from college and before he began his training to become an air force pilot. Almost as a lark, Jimmy went to work for a while with fifty other men and women cold calling for Prudential Brokerages in New York. On the first day Jimmy said he wasn't going to use the self-defeating script he was given, but rather one of his own (and my) devising, one that included a request to "tell me no." Okay, his manager said, but you'd better produce. Well, Jimmy did—about three times what anyone else in that office accomplished.

The Right to Say "No"

Many years ago I happened to be in Hong Kong after I'd just finished reading a book about negotiation that included a definition of "negotiation" pretty similar to the one from the book *Getting to Yes* quoted in my introduction. That definition was also a lot of words that don't say or mean much, when you consider them closely. Frustrated, and knowing that such thinking is worthless but without knowing exactly why, I stopped at a bookstore in Hong Kong and simply looked up "negotiation" in a dictionary. And there it was: "A negotiation is an agreement between two or more parties, with all parties having the right to veto."

These words struck me like a bolt of lightning. All these years later I remember the moment clearly. Eureka! A negotiation is simply an agreement between two or more parties, with all parties having the right to veto. That's what it is. Nothing more, nothing less, nothing fancy, nothing meaningless, nothing *win-win*.

Now, the right to veto is the right to say "no," isn't it? They're the same thing. As soon as I returned home, I tried a few experiments with the word "no" in harmless contexts. As a hobby, I had also started selling water softening systems for a guy I knew. My approach was simple: "Mrs. Smith, I have a little demonstration of what a water softener can do for you. Maybe it will interest you, maybe it won't. I don't know. If you'd like to look, I'd be happy to show you, and if you're interested, great, and if you're not, that's fine, too. I'll be on my way." Within months I was making more money selling water softening systems than I was flying jet airplanes. A big reason was my invitation to potential customers to tell me "no."

Okay, this is straightforward and uncontroversial enough, I believe, when we think about it, but it's a funny thing: in a negotiation, as we've seen, a simple "no" can be difficult to *say* in response to an offer and difficult to *hear* as a response to this offer. I suppose this ambivalence begins for each of us in our Terrible Twos, when we discover this incredible word. "NO!" gives us, for the first time in our lives, a little empowerment, but it also comes with the downside of battles with our parents, because "no" is a two-way street. We carry this experience with us the rest of our lives.

I said in chapter 1 that my admonition about neediness is probably the one principle of my system that has the most immediate beneficial impact on my clients. Now I should add that my "just say no" principle is the one that businesspeople find the *hardest* to truly accept and then put into practice. When they finally master the word the results are often magical, but for many it isn't easy to get over the hump. In the world of business, specifically, we are so immersed in the emotion-based atmosphere of win-win that saying "no" just sounds too harsh. It goes completely against the win-win grain of subservience and malleability and neediness. We all want to be liked, we don't want to hurt someone's feelings, we don't want to come across as too blunt or surly or arrogant or demanding, we don't want to shut the door on a deal prematurely, we don't want to start a win-win negotiation on a negative note. Therefore we pull our punches and say "maybe" or even "yes" and believe that this solves everyone's problem. We haven't had to say the nasty word and our adversary hasn't had to hear it. Win-win! No. Lose-lose, because we're stuck in our emotions and then get victimized *by* our emotions.

As Exhibit A I now introduce a client from some years ago, a lawyer and expert on Japanese business and legal practices who hired me because he could never get paid what he was worth. This was a man at the very top of his demanding field, a man who consulted with the prime minister of Japan, but he often worked for a $100 per hour consulting fee in the States. Just ridiculous. He should have received $400 minimum plus expenses, but he was a win-win negotiator, and he was always getting screwed, and he knew it, but he couldn't control himself. He certainly understood *in theory* the power of saying "no" and inviting the other party to say "no," but the idea of actually proceeding in this way on his own behalf was too terrifying. But one day we were driving together from San Francisco down to the Silicone Valley when he got a call on his mobile phone from a company wanting him to be an expert witness in Los Angeles for two days. On the spot, I urged him to take this opportunity to test the power of "no" for himself. He told the caller that he'd call right back, and we quickly came up with an agenda for him. (Agendas will be discussed in depth in chapter 12.) My client would ask for first-class airfare, a limousine at the airport, and $500 an hour, with a minimum of two days—a total of $8,000 for sixteen hours, to be transferred by wire immediately. There was nothing out of line about this proposal, nothing at all. For an expert of his prominence, he was right in line. Nevertheless, he was very uncomfortable when he returned the call, made his presentation, then invited them to say "no" if this was too much money. He would understand, he assured the other party, no hard feelings, and he was sure they could find another good expert witness somewhere on the West Coast. Maybe he could even recommend one, given a little time. So, he said, just let me know.

The caller on the other end said he'd have to check on this. My client hung up totally exhausted from his traumatic experience. Forty-five minutes later, the other party called back, agreed to the deal, and asked for the account number for the wire transfer.

Another client actually said to me recently, "How will people *like* my company if we don't cut our price?" In just so many words! He didn't ask, "How will my company be profitable?" or "How will we be seen as an effective, dynamic company with which to do business?" He asked, "How will they like me?"

This was a new and untrained client, that's for sure. He never thought in those terms again. Just imagine the predators out there lying in wait to take advantage of such a vulnerable adversary. Nevertheless, it's amazing how many negotiators want to be liked, want to *save* the adversary from making a tough decision. It happens every day. Here's another case in point. A few years ago, a client was dealing with a large Japanese corporation that had found itself in a tight situation that was shaping up to be very profitable to my client. A team of five negotiators was sitting in the room in Tokyo with a like number of counterparts for the Japanese company. The silence was deafening, as they say, and the damnedest thing happened: the burden for the adversary to make a decision became too much for one member of *my own team,* and he blurted out, then and there, with no consultation with his teammates, much less with his bosses back home, that the Japanese could have a 2 percent discount. Out of nowhere! And this was a billion-dollar negotiation. Two percent here, 2 percent there, and pretty soon you're talking about real money down the drain—all for the sake of making the adversary feel comfortable and saving them from taking responsibility for their decisions. The Japanese gladly accepted this offer, the meeting adjourned, all hell broke loose in the American camp, and the

team had to return to the table the following day and take back
that 2 percent discount, which they did.

Never "Save the Adversary" or "Save the Relationship"

Without question, one of the most dangerous mistakes you can
make in a negotiation is trying to "save the adversary," as I put it.
There can be no saving of the adversary emotionally, intellectually, financially, or on any level. No. None. Never. It's a terrible
practice that does neither side any good.

Neither side? That's correct, because if you do "save the adversary," *you* are now partially responsible for *their* decision. If some
problem comes up later, who gets the guilt trip laid on them?
Who sets himself up for another compromise? I hope the answer
is obvious. If it's not, consider this cautionary tale involving a
corporation in the microchip business and one of its major customers. Before I became involved in their negotiations, this
company had allowed one particular customer, a large multinational, to cancel a worldwide service contract. Specifically,
one man in the field allowed the supply system management guy
with the multinational to abrogate the agreement, because he
thought he could do better paying for maintenance and service
on a piecemeal basis. This was a terrible mistake by my client. In
the first place, the man in the field was negotiating with an unqualified adversary. He should never have allowed the purchasing
guy to make such a decision. The service agreement should have
been carefully looked at and renegotiated all the way up the line.
But in the name of friendship, my client's representative agreed
to kill the agreement. He had no idea what the ramifications

would be: when equipment finally started to require maintenance, the parts would require a week for delivery instead of a
day, and on-site service wouldn't be available 24/7, including
holidays. How could there be such blanket coverage?! It wasn't
being paid for. Nevertheless, when problems came up with
the piecemeal service, my client took the blame, even though it
was the other company's supply system management guy who
had asked for this new arrangement. Saving the adversary in
the name of friendship had backfired both for my client, who
ended up being the bad guy, and for the customer, who ended
up paying more for piecemeal service, when they factored in
downtime.

"Saving the adversary" is but one example of the many behaviors known in negotiating circles as "saving the relationship."
Some form of saving the relationship happens *hourly*, all over the
world, in all fields of endeavor. It's the whole idea behind win-
win. For example, a friend who works for a national touring
dance company was negotiating with the director of an organization that intended to bring the dance company to its venue.
But this director didn't want to sign the contract for the appearance, for reasons that were never made clear, and she enlisted the
aid of a colleague of my friend. This colleague blurted to my
friend, "I don't care if your position is logical! It's not a very nice
way to treat a major dance presenter!"

For fear of tarnishing his relationship with the adversary in
the negotiation, the colleague didn't want to appear too demanding. He didn't want to hurt the adversary's feelings by saying "no signed contract, no appearance by this dance company."
Because of his own deeply ingrained desire for approval, he was
unable to see the real problem in the negotiation. In effect, he

became nothing other than an in-house saboteur, prepared to put my friend and her dance company in the position of taking a considerable financial risk in order to save the relationship with the program director.

But that colleague was right about one thing: The program director did *not* appreciate hearing "no." She could not accept it when the booking agent said, "No, we are not coming to your town because we don't do business without a fully executed contract." In a thirty-minute phone monologue, the director said that in seventeen years of experience she had never been treated like this. She accused the agent of discounting her experience and reputation and integrity. She saw the agent's "no" as representing a lack of trust. She simply couldn't accept it.

This reaction is quite common, of course. In fact, in the early stage of a negotiation I'd say it's probably the most common reaction. People take "no" as personal rejection. They get ugly, they "go negative" in a big way. And this is why "saving the relationship" is classic win-win behavior. The unspoken—or sometimes spoken—assumption behind win-win is that people enter negotiations trying to build friendly relationships and want to leave with that relationship intact.

The classic win-win dilemma is this one: *How much money do I have to leave on the table in order to maintain this relationship?* Big-time corporate negotiators, along with many others, play this game to the hilt. They play up the importance of partnerships, loyalty, the long term—emotion-based stuff. *How could you endanger such benefits by holding the line?* But their only real concern is the price they're paying.

I've had a client say to me, "Oh, I'm good friends with their head of purchasing."

"Really? That's interesting."

"Yeah, his wife and my wife are pretty good friends, too. They play tennis."

"Really? How long have you had this relationship?"

"A couple of years, I guess."

"How long has he been head of purchasing?"

Pause. "A couple of years, I guess."

Welcome to more supply systems management, in which an explicit strategy is to use outings and junkets and any other means to establish friendships that can then be used as unspoken leverage when the adversary wants to say and should say "no" in the negotiation.

Friendships with the good folks on the other side can be fine—or they can be dangerous. It's hard enough for many negotiators to say "no" to adversaries they've just met. How much harder is it to say "no" to friends?

Respect, Not Friendship, Is What You Want

The impulse to think and act in any such save-the-relationship fashion is wrongheaded not only because it's bad negotiating, but also because the adversary across the table does *not* want to be a friend. Couldn't care less. *Has not even thought about it.* Now, I noted earlier in this chapter that most of us humans want to be liked, don't want to hurt feelings, don't want to be blunt or surly or arrogant. It's also true that we don't want to be on the *receiving* end of such behavior. But this does not mean that we want to be everybody's good friend. For businesspeople and negotiators in any field, much more important than friendliness are effectiveness and respect. Nothing more. Have you ever wondered how the jerks of the world get along? How some even get ahead?

How a very few even get to the top? These people don't get away with their boorish, offensive behavior for no good reason. They get away with it because they're effective in their work and bring benefit to their business relationships, in one way or another.

Every reader of this book understands exactly what I'm saying here. Every reader can think of a case in which she or he has chosen to deal with an obnoxious but effective person rather than a friendly but ineffective one. What does friendship have to do with making good business and negotiation decisions? Not a thing. As will become quite clear, I advocate and coach respectful dealings and politeness with the adversary at all times. This is mandatory for my clients. But this practice has nothing to do with *saving* the adversary from taking responsibility for decisions, all for the sake of friendship or for being liked or for feeling important. Most businesspeople, if they stop to think about this question carefully, will agree that friendships in business are the product of long-term effective dealings. Making decisions based on a sense that the adversary seeks your friendship is misguided. They would much prefer your effectiveness.

Why would you want to load down a business relationship with a lot of emotional baggage, including guilt, which can be the by-product of "friendship"? It doesn't work. It doesn't pay. If agreements result from effective decision making, the odds are very good that there will be a long-term business relationship, regardless whether you play golf with your adversary. If agreements are the result of ineffective decision making, there won't be—and should not be—a long-term relationship, no matter how many rounds you play.

The *Next* Decision

The fear of hurting people's feelings, of not being liked, of damaging a long-term relationship—these are all reasons we're afraid to say "no." Another is that we're afraid to make a *wrong* decision.

"No" is a pretty strong answer—a pretty strong decision—and what if it's the wrong one? People are terrified at the prospect, and this fear of the wrong decision is one of the most debilitating emotions of all, burrowing deep beneath all aspects of decision making. Inexperienced or wrongheaded negotiators believe that "no" locks them into a wrong decision and that "maybe" protects them from this wrong decision. We are paralyzed by doubt from all sides:

"Why take this deal?"
"The whole thing sounds too good."
"Maybe I can win even more."
"Why are they making this so easy?"
"What do they know that I don't know?"
"This can't be right."
"How can I get out of this?"

I or any businessperson could expand this list for pages. There's no doubt that the average negotiator is beset by doubt. The fear of making a wrong decision relates to all our fears of failing, which are deeply ingrained in most of us. In school we were afraid of giving a wrong answer because we'd look stupid and be laughed at by the other kids. In the business world, the wrong answer—the wrong decision—can have far worse ramifications. So we live in fear of that wrong decision, and that fear binds us. Unnecessary fear of a bad decision is a major stumbling block to good decisions.

How do you get rid of the fear of being wrong? I'll answer this question with another one: What really happens when we make a bad decision? We make another decision, and then another, and then another, and then another. A negotiation is a series of decisions. When—not if, but when—you make a bad decision, you simply follow it with a better one. Understanding this simple lesson will liberate you as a negotiator. Or as a flight instructor told my son during his training as a military pilot, "Lieutenant Camp, you sure make some bad decisions in this airplane, but don't worry. As long as you at least do make decisions, we can fix the bad ones."

Take responsibility for the bad decision, learn from it, embrace the failure, and soldier on without fear because you are only one decision away from getting back on track. But this attitude and approach take discipline and a lot of self-confidence, because being right is very important to most of us. It is a powerful *need,* and like all needs, it must be overcome.

In a negotiation with one of my clients, the adversary—a pretty big company with a famous set of initials—insisted on a 28 percent discount for the particular high-tech product in question. Even though this discounted price was barely breakeven for my client, the negotiator agreed to the demand. (When his boss found out, he called me with every intention of showing me the door—as he should have, except that I, too, had not been consulted about that giveaway.) That 28 percent giveback was a bad decision, a terrible decision, a killer decision. But it was *not* the end of the world. The following week my client went back to the adversary, reopened the negotiations, and told them he couldn't deliver at that price: "Sorry, but that agreement was a terrible mistake." In the end, the adversary agreed to forego most of that discount.

But wait a minute, wasn't the adversary therefore guilty of *saving* my client by renegotiating the agreed-to discount? I don't know; I wasn't privy to their internal considerations. They may have been saving us, or they may have made a careful business decision. I rather suspect the latter, because I'm talking about a careful company, but I can't prove it. Okay, but what if the company had said, "Tough. You negotiated the 28 percent discount, and we want it"? My client would have pulled the old negotiating team out of the picture, put in a new one, and the new team would have said, "Sorry, mea maxima culpa, we screwed up, but the machine is not coming at that deeply discounted price. Let's go from here."

And what would have happened then? We would have *negotiated*. But all too often, companies saddled with bad win-win contracts don't even consider renegotiation. Bad form, they say—and this is assuming they even understand that it *is* a bad contract, and they may not until the wolves are at the door. I've seen this many times.

Here are two classic cases from recent business annals about reversing terrible decisions. Some years ago Coca-Cola decided they needed to change their formula, and they came on the market with the "new Coke." A bad decision, a terrible decision, a killer decision, an unbelievably embarrassing decision. But it was not the end of the world. The company simply reversed the decision. (Or was that first decision actually an unbelievably *clever* marketing ploy? I've heard that theory, which holds that the company merely pretended to replace Coke Classic with New Coke in order to remind us how much we love the Real Thing.

Either way—blunder or ploy—things worked out well, because sales soared, along with the company's capitalization, which has gone from $9 billion to something closer to $100 billion since 1985.)

Then we have another giant, Microsoft, which was dead wrong for years in its dismissive attitude toward the Internet. When Bill Gates realized his error, he turned his giant company of fifteen thousand employees on a dime. Within ninety days, every division of Microsoft re-envisioned its purpose in terms of the Net. Whatever your feelings about Gates, you have to ac-knowledge that this was an incredible demonstration of business leadership. He wasn't going to persevere in a bad decision (or a nondecision, actually). He did an about-face, and nobody thinks the less of him for it.

One Last Time

Embrace "no" at every opportunity in a negotiation. Don't fear the word, invite it. You do *not* take it as a personal rejection be-cause you are not needy. You understand that every "no" is *re-versible.* The moment you really internalize this principle of the Camp System, you will be a much better negotiator. The moment you quit worrying about whether you will hurt someone's feelings, the moment you quit trying to save your adversary, you will be a much better negotiator. The moment you understand the honesty and the *power* of "no" you will have taken a long stride away from emotion-based negotiating and toward deci-sion-based negotiating.

If you cannot accept "no," you will burn too many bridges and have no way back into too many negotiations. Nothing—*absolutely nothing*—is more important to a successful negotiation than for you to make as clear as posssible from the very beginning that "no" is a perfectly acceptable response at this negotiating table. You must make clear that you do not take "no" as a personal rejection, but as an honest decision that can be discussed and perhaps reversed. You must make clear that a blunt "no" is preferable to "maybe," which tells you nothing at all, and also preferable to "yes," a total nonstarter. You must challenge the niceties of the emotion-based win-win system that accomplish nothing, at best, or set you up for a sucker, more likely.

This can be difficult to do when dealing with committed win-win adversaries, but when you are able to do so, you'll be amazed how this right to say and hear "no" clears the air at the negotiating table. If your adversary is a shrewd, highly trained expert, they'll consider you with a great deal more respect. If your adversary is a naive win-winner, they will feel much more safe. They can give you an honest "no," you'll accept it gratefully, and they know you'll react in the same way in the future. Feeling safe saying "no," they also feel safe hearing "no." Barriers go down, trust goes up, everyone feels more comfortable, everyone becomes more forthright, we're all adults here, the atmosphere of honesty is welcome.

In the long run, "no" is really the safest answer. It does *not* tear down business relationships. It *builds* them. You want win-win? Saying and inviting and hearing "no" are the real win-win.

4

Success Comes from This Foundation

Develop Your Mission and Purpose

EFFECTIVE NEGOTIATION IS effective decision making, plain and simple, and the foundation of effective decision making is a valid mission and purpose to guide it. This is bedrock in my system. How can you stay on track during a long negotiation or endeavor of any kind without a clear mission and purpose? There's no other way. But if you do develop and adhere to a valid mission and purpose, how can you go off the track? It's impossible. If you have a valid mission and purpose, and the result of your negotiation fulfills this mission and purpose, it's a good and worthwhile negotiation.

Now, that's pretty simple. It doesn't sound all that profound, but the principle works like magic. It's an airtight guide for effective decision making.

Remember from the previous chapter that list of doubts that

disrupt effective decision making? Here it is again (and it could
have been a lot longer):

> *"Why take this deal?"*
> *"The whole thing sounds too good."*
> *"Maybe I can win even more."*
> *"Why are they making this so easy?"*
> *"What do they know that I don't know?"*
> *"This can't be right."*
> *"How can I get out of this?"*

Forget all this stuff! If your negotiation serves a valid mission
and purpose, you don't have to worry about whether you *get*
every last dollar or concession out of the deal, or whether you
gave enough dollars and concessions. You don't worry about the
long-term relationship. You are not responsible for the other
party's decisions. You don't care whether this contract is win-
win, win-lose, lose-win, or lose-lose. Such *scorekeeping* is suddenly seen for what it is: arbitrary, empty, meaningless. You don't
have to worry about it anymore, and this freedom will liberate
you in a negotiation, believe me.

I teach and I *preach* that mission and purpose is the very
essence of success. It must become as automatic as breathing.
You must develop the habit of referring to it on matters great
and small, because it gives you crystal-clear guidance in all cases.
The ultimate example of the effectiveness of the mission and
purpose to guide decisions in the most difficult and critical circumstances imaginable—so difficult and critical that they're
unimaginable, really, to my mind—was President Lincoln's
single-minded focus on saving the Union. That was his mission
and purpose in his negotiation with his constituency and his *other*
negotiation with the Confederacy: save the Union. At any cost.

Lincoln had decided that the dream of a North American continent that could avoid the precedent offered by the European
states—war after war after war—would be so jeopardized should
the Union break apart that he was willing to make any personal
sacrifice (which he did, in the end, and not to his surprise), and
he was willing to *ask* any sacrifice of his people, including this
Civil War, in the service of that mission and purpose.

As the general of the Union troops in the Civil War, Ulysses S.
Grant adhered without hesitation to Lincoln's mission and purpose of saving the Union by any means necessary, including horrible losses on the battlefield. Grant sacrificed his troops before
the Confederate barricades at Vicksburg and Spotsylvania and
Cold Harbor and Petersburg because he understood that his superior numbers and equipment would win the war of attrition
in the end. But as a *president,* Grant was a failure, taking bad advice, making bad decisions, dealing with a host of unsavory
characters, mainly because he didn't know why he was president
and what he hoped to accomplish during Reconstruction. He
didn't have a clear mission and purpose.

What great decision, what great achievement, was accomplished without the valid M&P? Certainly there have been acci-
dental discoveries in technology, but again, I ask you, what great
political or scientific or social or philanthropic deed, or what
work of art, was pulled off without the focus, control, and reso-
lution provided by a clear mission and purpose? I don't believe
you can name one. Another favorite illustration I use in my
workshops is the example of Thomas Alva Edison, who could
have settled for putting up one streetlight as a demonstration of
his technology, or who could have wired the world's first electric
toaster, but he hewed to his mission and purpose—adopting
electrical energy for the everyday use of mankind—and invested

an astronomical amount of his own money in order to light up an entire block in New York City. What a great story. What a great vision. What a great mission and purpose.

How many decisions will make things tougher today than they were yesterday but benefit you dramatically in the long term? I often use the example of the hypothetical inventor who can invest his life savings either in a marketing campaign for his product or in a complicated, expensive patent application on which there won't be a decision for three to five years. Without a valid mission and purpose he might go astray, think short term, and go to the market without a patent. But what happens if the product does take off and he hasn't protected the invention? He has lost in both the short *and* the long terms. With a valid mission and purpose he wouldn't make that mistake. He'd file for that patent.

Another, more practical story involves a storyteller and artist with a successful business in the Midwest. This client lived in a small town and had the opportunity to become involved with all sorts of businesses, some directly related to his native talents and aspirations, some pretty far-fetched in that regard. He had acquired a copy shop, a print shop, and an Internet service provider, to name just a few of his enterprises. Clearly, he is a very bright guy with a lot of energy, and if an opportunity seemed pretty good, he dived right in. After a few years, his became the classic situation of overreaching. He had failed to stick to his knitting, as Grandmom used to say. This happens a lot, of course. Someone starts out selling ice cream cones, then starts making the ice cream, then buys his own cows—and then figures he might as well open a butcher shop as well!

First things first, I said to my new client, and he got to

work on his mission and purpose, and this is what he determined:

My mission and purpose is to help people see, discover, and decide to experience this world as a world of imagination and possibility and healing. We do this by sharing our stories and the model of our company, in a way that is sustainable now and into the future our children will inherit.

Once he put this valid mission and purpose in place, my client could see clearly which of his subsidiary companies made sense. Once he had this clear vision, the decisions about what to keep and what to divest were easy enough. For years now he has done very well for himself and for many others by adhering to the spirit of this statement in all his businesses and negotiations.

Throughout these pages you will see how negotiators and companies who have a valid mission and purpose in place, one which clearly expresses their long-term aim and continuing responsibility, are able to handle any contingency that may come up in the daily give-and-take of their businesses. Their decision-making abilities are tenfold more powerful than those of negotiators operating on a wing and a prayer. Supply system management adversaries will fire in your direction a veritable fusillade of promises, threats, requests, deadlines, quibbles, position papers, and other stuff. Mission and purpose will serve as your very own missile defense shield to deal with these tactics.

Example: At the request of one of the biggest chipmakers in the world, my client provided a complete, in-depth, across-the-board proposal for selling about $50 million worth of the boxes that carry the silicon chips along the production line in the factory. (I should explain that these are not just any boxes. They're not corrugated paper, that's for sure, but high-tech in the extreme. They can cost almost $3,000 apiece.) Four other companies in the world make these boxes; all had prepared proposals for the giant chipmaker. A great deal of negotiation had been required in order for my client to understand exactly what the customer required, but after receiving this comprehensive, carefully negotiated proposal, the supply system management team at the chipmaker tried to break out the pieces of the proposal and negotiate them separately. Why? To induce compromise, of course.

My client declined to do this. Its mission and purpose was to provide the highest level of technology for the 300 mm arena, as it's known, while minimizing to the extent possible the risk of failure for the chipmaker. With this M&P in place, and given the fact that the elements of their proposal had been crafted to work *in tandem* to minimize the risk of failure for the chipmaker, my client simply couldn't agree to break their proposal into pieces, because this would have undermined their M&P.

Of course, the supply system management people with the chipmaker weren't thinking in these terms. They saw their job as saving money *up front*. So the crux of the negotiation revolved around getting the *real* decision makers at the chipmaker (the challenge of finding the real decision makers is the subject of chapter 11) to focus on the risk involved in using an inferior box, which was huge, because the failure of a single one at just the right place and just the right time in the production line can cost millions of dollars.

In the end, that chipmaker saw the light, awarded the contract to my client, and paid full price.

Mission and purpose is just as important for negotiations in our private lives as in our businesses and careers. I'm thinking of another client, the proud and happy father of a premature baby girl born with a defective heart valve—a condition, the parents were told, that many premature babies are born with. Sometimes this valve can be induced to close with drugs, but if not, surgery is required. In the case of my client's baby, the drugs failed. The doctors wanted to move her to another hospital for the required surgery, the hospital where the best pediatric thoracic surgeons practiced. The parents—my client and his wife—saw no reason for this move. The hospital their daughter was in had a state-of-the-art neonatal unit. In addition, there was an operating theater attached to the neonatal unit. They feared that transferring their daughter to another hospital was too much of a risk to take. But my client, a veteran businessman and negotiator, also knew he was too emotional to talk to the doctors and to argue his feelings effectively.

This was a negotiation, pure and simple, and my client developed the specific mission and purpose of getting the head of the neonatal unit to see and decide that he was risking the baby's life by transferring her to another hospital. Having this idea in place guided what the parents said to the doctor and how they said it. It helped them keep their emotions in check, and this in turn prevented the doctors from lumping them—understandably enough, perhaps—into the category of emotionally overwrought parents who don't have to be taken seriously. The mission and purpose did its job in guiding the interview with the doctors, although the eventual decision was a surprise. We'll see exactly how, and why, in chapter 9.

What happens if you *don't* have a valid mission and purpose in place? I've learned that a surefire way to get everyone's attention is to answer that question this way: If you're not working on behalf of your own mission and purpose, you're working on behalf of someone else's. That gives everyone pause. Now, it's fine to work on behalf of someone else if you understand that you are doing so—if you freely embrace and take their mission and purpose as your own or build your own to support theirs—but it is a terrible waste to work on behalf of someone else's mission and purpose without realizing it. But if you don't have one, haven't even thought about the subject, that's what is happening. People who are unhappy and frustrated in their work either have invalid mission and purposes—"I want to make a million dollars before I'm twenty-one"—or they don't have one and are serving someone else's, and some part of them understands this at some deep level.

I know and have worked with quite a few freelancers and sole proprietors and owners of very small businesses who feel that their mission and purpose is self-evident. This was a mistake for my client in the Midwest, and it's a mistake for anyone in his position. The mission and purpose is not self-evident. If you work for yourself and do not have one in place, you are working at a great disadvantage. You're just as vulnerable to working and negotiating on behalf on an invalid mission and purpose as is an employee at a giant, faceless multinational corporation. You must begin to develop one immediately. Now let's see how to do this.

Money and Power Are Not Valid

I want to make a million dollars before I'm twenty-one.
I want to make 10 million dollars this year.
I want to leave a legacy of 100 million dollars.
I want to become president and CEO of this company.
I want to be the most powerful politician in the state.
XYZ is committed to increasing sales this year by 25 percent.

These are some popular mission and purpose statements, if not stated quite so bluntly. This is how a lot of people and employees construe their life's and their company's work. Already, at this early point in the book, I imagine readers know the negative opinion I hold about all such statements, but the essential problem is not that these are narrow, shortsighted goals. The essential problem is that they are *I-centered*. They are set in the world of the individual building the mission and purpose. This is why they are 100 percent *invalid* and worthless for any person, business, or negotiation. I have nothing against money and power properly acquired and used, but they must be the *result,* not the essence, of a valid mission and purpose.

History and experience should tell each and every one of us, time and time again, that having wealth and/or power as the aim in life will destroy any individual (and many other people, in some instances). The cliché is worth repeating one more time: Money for money's sake does corrupt; power for power's sake does corrupt. Will businesspeople whose mission and purpose is to "make a killing" grow and thrive in the long run with such a narrow, self-serving mission and purpose? It is no more possible for them than it was for Hitler or Ferdinand Marcos or Joseph Stalin.

One of the great American business tragedies of the 1980s was the death of Eastern Airlines. Time has shown that Eastern didn't die. It was killed by its leadership and some junk-bond guys. I'm sure these men could have presented a mission and purpose for public consumption that addressed jobs and lower ticket prices for the consumer and safety in the air, but the *real* M&P seemed to have been to strip the airline of its assets, leaving only bills and debt for the creditors.

Perhaps the best case in point from more recent business annals is that of Quaker Oats and Snapple. The giant corporation bought the drink company for about $1.7 billion in 1994, believing that there would be a good fit between Snapple and their Gatorade brand. But Snapple had a completely different kind of distribution plan than Quaker Oats used for Gatorade, and the company's plan to force Snapple's distributors and buyers into conforming to the Gatorade model were resisted and eventually failed. A few years after Snapple was bought for the $1.7 billion, it was sold by Quaker Oats for about $300 million. The acquiring company, TriArc, knew what it was doing, rebuilt the brand, and sold it for $1.6 billion to Cadbury Schweppes—and they didn't even need that, since they were on the road show for their IPO when that offer came in.

When I read about such acquisition debacles, of which there are many every year, I automatically analyze the deal in terms of valid versus invalid mission and purpose. On the surface, bringing Snapple and Gatorade under the same umbrella made sense, but the valid mission and purpose isn't just on the surface, and it doesn't suppose that the company that sells one popular drink can *necessarily* sell another one.

What about the predatory negotiators I have warned about who sound like the kind of people who would have "make a killing" as their mission and purpose? Well, maybe it is their M&P, but not necessarily. Their predatory negotiating is a means; they're simply taking advantage of weak win–win negotiators. They might have a perfectly valid mission and purpose. In any event, I don't blame the predatory negotiators. I blame the weak win–win negotiators who feed them.

Another problem with concentrating on money and power as a mission and purpose is that you're scorekeeping, and scorekeeping means you're thinking about results over which you have no real control. To repeat, you're thinking about breaking par for the first time (or bogey, more likely), not about the requirements of this crucial shot on seventeen. You're thinking about the new Beemer, not about the discipline and hard work you'll need in the negotiation that, if it's successful, will ultimately pay for that shiny new car. And one final point here, just to set the record straight. The great coach Vince Lombardi of the Green Bay Packers did say, for commercial purposes, "Winning isn't everything, it is the only thing," but when I heard him address the football team at Ohio State during spring practice in 1965, I believe, he put the point somewhat differently: "Winning isn't everything, but the will to prepare to win is everything." I trust the distinction between the two statements is clear. I also believe that the second statement must have reflected Lombardi's true feelings, because a great coach of any sport or any endeavor at all knows that the first attitude guarantees failure, sooner or later, because winning is beyond our control, while preparation is 100 percent under our control. And what is the cornerstone of preparation? Mission and purpose.

Your M&P Is Set in Your *Adversary's* World

Make that a *valid* mission and purpose. What is a valid M&P? First and foremost, it must be set *in the adversary's world*. For a politician and leader, it must be set in the world of his or her constituents. For a businessperson, it must be set in the world of the customer. For a negotiator, it must be set in the world of the team sitting across the table. Setting the mission and purpose in the constituents' or the customer's or the adversary's world allows all of them to see clearly the features and benefits that you and your product or service have to offer them. For the negotiator, setting the mission and purpose statement in the adversary's world is a fundamental way in which you see your adversary's world clearly and without false assumptions, and get the adversary to see and act with the same clarity.

> *My mission and purpose is to help people see, discover, and decide to experience this world as a world of imagination and possibility and healing. We do this by sharing our stories and the model of our company, in a way that is sustainable now and into the future our children will inherit.*

When you read the artist's mission and purpose a few pages back, perhaps you noticed something different about it but didn't stop at the time to pin down this difference. Now's the time. Please take a minute or two to study the statement and absorb the fact that it's fundamentally, irrevocably set in the world of his customer. It has nothing whatsoever to do with buying more businesses or making more money, and not because he's playing games with words. He isn't. Recently this client told me, "Mission and purpose is what I stand for in the world—above all, what I want to accomplish and how I want to accomplish it. If it came to the hour of my death, I could say wholeheartedly that this is something that I am willing to live for."

Recall my client who was about to meet with the doctors concerning his baby girl. His mission and purpose was to get the head of the neonatal unit to see and decide that he was risking the baby's life by transferring her to another hospital. It was set in the world of the doctors. In a valid mission and purpose, our world must be secondary. You might understandably ask why, if it's *my* mission and purpose, do I want to focus on someone else? Because unless you live alone on a desert island, your mission and purpose *is* to focus on someone else. That "someone else" is your lifeblood, whether you're a politician, a doctor, a patient, a businessperson, or a negotiator. Don't ever forget this. As a negotiator, you don't go *anywhere* without your adversary, by definition.

We all know the phrase that is now de rigueur in retail sales: "The customer comes first." I'd like to know the retail company that has thrived over a long period of time with any other modus operandi. This is the reason I wonder about the long-term prospects for companies that take advantage of booms and let their customer service slide. The airlines come to mind, judging by the number of complaints pouring in to the FAA. Other companies that have theoretically modernized their customer service with those automated phone programs that serve mainly to enrage us with their endless loops may be in for a surprise when things cool off. There will be some winners and losers, and I know whom I'm betting on.

Over the long haul, you put profits in the bank by putting the customer first, and there's a direct analogy with negotiation: We greatly enhance our opportunity for a successful deal by putting the adversary first in our mission and purpose. You make your killing—or just a solid profit—only by entering heart and soul into your adversary's world, business, needs, requirements, hopes, fears, and plans. Your mission and purpose is to allow her or him to see and decide that you build and service the best machine for the task at a competitive price. It is *not* to sell ten thousand machines this fiscal year. By providing the best machine, you may sell the ten thousand, but focusing on them is putting the profit before the performance, your world before your adversary's. It won't work.

Recall now the company on the brink of bankruptcy because it was losing $100,000 with every shipment. Cutting costs was not an issue here; costs were not the problem. The problem was that the company had been taken to the cleaners in the negotiation with its primary customer. It had allowed the price to be driven to below-cost levels. Let's examine some possible M&Ps for a company in this dire situation.

"Renegotiate this contract." Well, this company certainly did want to renegotiate the big contract.

"Become profitable again." Management, employees, and shareholders certainly did want it to become profitable again.

But those approaches would never work, because they did not address the world of the other company with which it had the fateful contract, and which was under no obligation to renegotiate the contract. Instead of those two self-centered statements, the company developed the following customer-centered mission and purpose for the upcoming renegotiation:

> *To help [the other company's] management at the very highest level see our company as a new and revitalized organization that is going to change its effectiveness to the benefit not only of their company but also to that of the whole industry by becoming a more effective and competent supplier to that industry.*

And they were able to accomplish this mission.

Remember our high school athlete deciding among colleges in chapter 3? His mission and purpose was not "get into a good program so I'll be recruited by the pros and sign for five million." He wasn't going to be a pro, and he knew it. Nor was his M&P "to get into a top academic school so I can make lots of money after I graduate." Nor was it "to get as far away as possible from home." The last two might have been considerations, but all would have been invalid missions and purposes because all were set in his world. His *valid* mission and purpose was to provide the coaches with an individual who would put forth the effort required for complete team success. Likewise, the mission and purpose of the booking agent for the dance company in the negotiation with the program director was not to secure another week of touring for the company and increase its earnings. It was not to secure a commission for the booking agent and increase her earnings. It was to get this director to see and decide that presenting this particular dance company would bring cultural richness to her organization's audiences and community, and to help the program director fulfill her organization's own mission and purpose.

As an interviewee for a job, your mission and purpose might be to help the employer see and decide that you are a person of great character and integrity that the employer's company must have in order to take its business to a new level. As a Realtor it might be to help the seller see and decide that it is in *her* best long-term interest that she accept this offer that she is able to secure from you today. As a commercial plumber, it might be to help contractors see and decide that you bring great benefit to their projects by providing professional workmanship, using the highest-quality supplies and materials available, and guaranteeing on-time completion. As a travel agent, it might be to help travelers see and decide that your knowledge and experience in the field and attention to detail would enhance every aspect of their travel.

And what about Jim Camp, book author? My mission and purpose is to provide the opportunity for people to elevate their level of success, accomplishing this by means of clear, concise writing that presents in a systematic way the keys to decision-based negotiating. When I asked some of my clients about the wisdom of this project, a couple wondered aloud whether I could do the job sufficiently in a single book. Confronted by this doubt, I returned to my mission and purpose and thought about the key word, which is "opportunity."

My purpose here isn't to elevate your success regardless, but simply to provide you with the *opportunity* to do so. A huge difference, obviously, and I have no doubt at all that this book does provide that opportunity, and so I am writing it.

In 1999, Major League Baseball umpires must have thought their mission and purpose was to show the lords of baseball that they couldn't get along without the umpires. Bad thinking. They were blinded by their incorrect assessment, and some of them paid with their jobs. Their mission and purpose should have been to get the players, the fans, and the lords of the game to see and decide that the umpires provide the highest level of expertise in calling balls and strikes and plays at the bases while remaining invisible on the field. Something like this: "Invisible" is important, I think, because I've played a lot of baseball, and used to umpire Pony League games, and I know how easy it is for the ump to slip into a power trip. A mission and purpose including invisibility would well serve the umpires and referees in all sports.

With such an M&P, why would you go on strike, which is, by definition, a high-visibility act? What would have happened if the umpires had said instead that they would *never* go out on strike, because that would damage the game all of us love, but that they *would* work hard to alert the players and the fans of their situation, that they would hire a public relations firm to that end? I think the negotiation might have turned out differently.

Of course, I'm shooting from the hip here. I wasn't privy to the details of that episode, and I don't know for sure how I would have coached either the umpires or the owners, had they been my clients, but I do know that the umpires, surely, and maybe also the owners were flailing around without a valid mission and purpose.

They were not alone. Invalid mission and purposes are at the heart of many labor disputes, almost by definition.

By now, the phrase "see and decide" in most of the mission and purpose statements presented above must be obvious. Why this phrase? Often, you want to create a *vision* in the other party that will move them to take *action*. Mission and purpose drives vision for all parties, and vision drives effective decision making for all parties. It's as simple as that. In short, you may want your adversaries *to see and decide*. From what perspective will they see and decide? From the perspective of their own world, of course. Therefore your mission and purpose must be set in their own world—the key criterion for a valid M&P.

There are other criteria as well. All good mission and purpose statements are concise. If we can state our mission and purpose simply and concisely, we can create the vision we want. If we get too complicated, too convoluted, we cloud the vision. Even if such statements are valid, they make creating a vision difficult.

The mission and purpose must always be written. What happens when you go through the process of writing anything down? I can't tell you, technically, but I do know that putting a thought in writing makes it stronger and reinforces commitment. Our mind is an amazing thing, but it can lose focus. Important matters are written down for a reason, and it's not to create busywork. So pick up your pen or sit down at the keyboard.

This is the day and age of teamwork in business, and the team must have its own mission and purpose that is in complete support of the overall mission and purpose of the institution. Everybody has to be on the same page, and happily so. With a team, the mission and purpose has to be *negotiated*—and in a negotiation, all parties have the right to say no, of course.

You may also have realized by now that an individual or a company may have *more than one* mission and purpose. The company renegotiating the contract on which it was losing $100,000 on every machine delivered developed a specific mission and purpose for the renegotiation.

You or your company may well have many M&Ps, because you have one for almost every major task you undertake, and for many seemingly minor tasks as well. You have the overall mission and purpose for your business or enterprise. You have a second mission and purpose for your negotiation with a specific adversary. Within that negotiation you have yet other layers of mission and purpose, each of which guides the decision making at that point. In complicated, high-stakes negotiations, my clients may have a written mission and purpose for almost every phone call to anyone on the other side. No kidding. And each, of course, is set in the world of the adversary.

And one more thing about mission and purpose, which may at first blush sound completely contradictory to every previous point in this chapter. Your mission and purpose can and perhaps should *change*. If you're a plumber, the skills and attributes you bring to your work may not change, so your mission and purpose might not, either. But it might if, say, the emphasis of your business switched from residential to commercial. We can easily see how the situation of an individual with a less clearly focused business, like real estate, might change. In any event, if the features and benefits that you bring to the table do change, you will have a different vision of what can be accomplished, and your mission and purpose should change accordingly. Earlier in this chapter I referred to Ulysses S. Grant's victory as a Civil War general but failure as a president. Another way to look at that career is that Grant had the mission and purpose for the Civil War but was unable to develop one for his Reconstruction presidency. One could analyze George Bush's reelection defeat in 1992 as a failure to convince the electorate that he had a new mission and purpose for a post–Gulf War America. In 2000, Al Gore lost the election in large part, I believe, because he, like many vice presidents who run for the presidency, wasn't quite able to develop and sell his own M&P, one independent from Bill Clinton's.

Think about how the Internet has changed the products and services that phone companies offer their customers, that catalog companies offer their customers, or that advertising companies offer their customers. I've already mentioned how Bill Gates finally saw the light regarding the Internet and changed Microsoft's mission and purpose in three months. The Internet has or should have changed the mission and purpose of most of the businesses in this economy. In the end, who will be immune to it?

A Valid M&P Will Never Let You Down

In his excellent book *Management: Tasks, Responsibilities, and Practices,* Peter Drucker dedicates many pages to the issue of understanding what it is you *really* do—your mission and purpose. He writes, "Your business is never apparent. It requires in-depth questioning that gives you a process that provides constant refocusing of what you do." You must continuously analyze and ask yourself: What is my business? What is my mission? What is my purpose? As you set a valid mission and purpose in place, you will discover that the picture of what you are trying to accomplish becomes crystal clear and you eliminate all confusion. As a negotiator, once you have a mission and purpose you can control your emotions, you can make effective decisions. If every decision you make—even one that doesn't turn out well—is in the service of a sound mission and purpose, you cannot go wrong, not in the long run.

How many ways can I say it? Mission and purpose can be the most powerful single card you hold in your hand.

5

Stop Trying to
Control the Outcome

Focus on Your Behavior
and Actions Instead

S OME YEARS AGO, I was unwinding with one of my best and
most successful students at the time, a salesman, and he told
me the following story:

> *"You know, Jim, I have a prospect in my area that I called on for*
> *more than two years. Around 8:30 in the morning on the first*
> *Monday of each month I'd stop by and see him—a really nice guy,*
> *but I thought he would never buy from me. He always seemed unable*
> *to focus on the issues. To tell the truth, it was frustrating, and I only*
> *called on him because he was so close to where I lived. It was conve-*
> *nient. He was part of my monthly plan. One week I was on my way*
> *home one afternoon, with a little time to spare. I decided to stop by*
> *and see this man. And he was a different guy! He was focused, he ac-*
> *knowledged he had some problems we could fix, and he gave me my*

*first order right then. I was shocked. After we finished the paperwork
I had to ask him, 'Why today?' What had brought him to buy from
me on that day? He said, 'Well, I'm diabetic and it takes me a couple hours in the morning to get my blood sugar under control. I have
trouble getting started until about ten in the morning. Come to think
of it, I don't think I ever place an order until the afternoon, probably
out of habit. I appreciate your continuing to come and see me.' "*

Ouch. Two years! In chapter 8 we'll look at the mistake my
client made that caused this negotiation to take that long in the
first place, but the point for our discussion now is that not one of
those visits was wasted time, and this would have been true even
if he hadn't eventually signed the deal.

Our subject now is goals. Just as with mission and purpose, I
believe in these tools but call for a very different approach from
the usual one. My clients do *not* set sales targets, quotas, numbers, percentages. Never. Instead, they set goals they can control.

So, what can we control? If you're able to answer this question and really internalize that answer, you're way ahead of most
people, including many "professional" negotiators. When I ask
this question in workshops and seminars, only a few people will
answer, "Ourselves." This is the correct answer, but only partially. Can we manage our heart rate, for example? I've read that
certain monks of a high caliber can do so, but most of us cannot.
Can we control our anger following an insult? Not really, not the
emotion itself. Time? Can we control time? Well, we can't alter
the fact that there are only twenty-four hours a day to work
with, and some of these will be "lost" to sleep, but we can control what we do during our waking hours and how we do it. By
this progression we arrive at the real answer to what we can con-

trol about ourselves: *behavior and activity,* or as I sometimes put it, *an action or effort to an end.*

Your anger following an insult is not under your control, but your behavior is. You decide whether to strike back in some way or to turn the other cheek. In your life, in your negotiations, you develop habits of behavior, good and bad, and you have activities that you pursue that help or hinder you. Everything else—everything, *including all results*—we might as well think of as acts of God.

If my client's goal had been "to sell his product" to his diabetic customer, he would have given up. But that would never have been his goal, because the actual sale was an end over which he had no control, and no one in his right mind would set a goal over which he had no control.

Or would he? Of course he would! It happens all the time in the business world, and in our private lives as well. I'd even say that most companies, professionals, and individuals set performance goals that are really *results,* over which they have no control and which they fail to meet time after time after time. I have spent years in front of thousands of negotiators in straight sales, men and women who may earn $750,000 a year in commissions, students in college preparing for their first real job, top executives of Fortune 500 companies. I have coached the negotiations of some of the most successful service and academic institutions in the world. Invariably, no matter the background, all of these good people want the same thing: results! But when I ask them to identify the behaviors and activities required of their negotiation or sales teams, they don't know. They can't do it. All they know is that on every sales team there is—and has to be, by definition—the top seller or the top negotiator, no matter the market condition, no matter the difficulty of the negotiation. Why can't everyone deliver results like that?!

Well, many more of us can, but only if we understand the difference between a goal and a result, between what we can and cannot control.

Control What You Can Control, Forget the Rest

What goals did you set prior to sitting down with this book and thinking at greater length about the art and science of negotiation? You probably didn't set any. That's fine. Most people wouldn't; no one said you had to. But I suggest that *now* you think about your goal for this undertaking. If I were a beginner in the study of decision-based negotiation (as opposed to emotion- and compromise-based negotiation), my initial goals would be to focus at all times on my mission and purpose, to control my neediness and never demonstrate neediness, to always allow my adversary to be okay, to have no fear of saying or hearing "no"—the subjects of the preceding chapters. Right there you have four very straightforward, obtainable, valid goals that, if carefully followed, would make you an excellent negotiator, relative to the field. But the real point I want to get across here is the distinction between a goal and a result (or objective, as it's commonly labeled). Goals you can control, objectives you cannot. By following your behavioral goals, you get to your objectives.

One last time: instead of trying to break par (or bogey, more likely), a result we cannot control, we concentrate on putting a good swing on the ball, an action we can control. The distinction is crystal clear, surely, but it never ceases to amaze me that the same folks in my workshops who nod their heads in agreement with the golf analogy turn right around and announce that their goal in this negotiation is to sign the deal and collect the money.

So I ask you again, is this signing and collecting something that you can actually manage and control? You can attempt to influence someone else's decision, to help them see, but can you manage the final decision itself? Not if this is a genuine negotiation in which both parties have the right to say "no." You cannot forge the adversary's signature. Or think about it this way: After you've led the horse to the water, can you make it drink? The old adage says no, and the old adage is right.

As you work through these lessons and apply them to your business and your life, you'll develop a keen awareness of exactly what you can and cannot control, and therefore what is and is not a valid goal. What you can control is behavior and activity, what you cannot control is the result of this behavior and activity.

Think behavior, forget result. Should someone exhort you, "Go get 'em, gang! Make something happen! Stir the pot! Go for the jugular! Close, close, close!" you should ignore this yelling and screaming. If you think this individual is worth the effort, you should point out why these are not valid goals. And if you don't think this individual is worth the effort but you're stuck with him or her as a manager or colleague, you should think seriously about a new venue for your labors, because at this one you'll be wasting time, effort, and money.

Even if some kind of quantitative goal is achieved, it is *still* an invalid, dangerous goal. Say you're a salesperson and you've "got your number" for the week, and it's only Wednesday. You might be tempted to think, *Man, I'm great. I'll relax the rest of the week. It's my reward.* See the problem? Worse, what if you don't have your number toward the end of the week? You tend to work *harder,* not *smarter,* all in the service of what's not valid anyway. You end up working on the wrong problem or with the wrong activities and habits and dig a deeper hole. And if you're into the win-win thing, you very likely end up making a classic win-win mistake: the unnecessary compromise in the course of chasing an invalid goal. That's a killer.

In my negotiation coaching experience—and it's pretty broad, ranging over many different fields of business—I have seen that the failure to set manageable goals is as common a mistake as any other. People get confused because they don't have a step-by-step plan. They casually talk about goals and results, or objectives, but they don't really know how to distinguish between them. For one thing, they don't have a mission and purpose to guide them. They thereby put themselves on an emotional roller coaster, and this is a fatal error, as we shall see time and again in these pages. Disappointment, excitement, despair, hope—they experience the whole range of emotions, and all because they're reacting to events over which they don't have control and ignoring those over which they do have control.

By following your valid goals you obtain your objective. By obtaining your objective you further your mission and purpose. At all times you set goals and objectives that are as valid as the mission and purpose they serve. It sounds simple, and it is simple to state and to understand, but it takes discipline and practice to actually live and negotiate in this way. You could think of my system—and this book—as nothing more or less than a means to identify activities and behaviors that we can control during a negotiation.

The Negotiation Never Ends

When does a negotiation really end? Conventional wisdom holds that it ends when the deal is put to bed, when the paper is signed, before the ink has even dried. But if this were true, we would never encounter buyer's remorse, would we? We wouldn't need lawyers (or as many lawyers). Customers wouldn't change suppliers, suppliers wouldn't decide they don't want anything to do with that customer again. In the real world, the negotiation does not end when the paper is signed. Tough negotiators for the multinationals—supply systems management types—operate under the *assumption* that contracts are easily broken, that this is just part of business, and that their corporations have more legal staying power than the smaller businesses they're dealing with.

Take just a minute to think back on some of your most critical negotiations, either in your business or private life. Did they really end, or did they keep going? Some of them kept going, I know that. Now, how did you react? If your goal had been "to sign the deal," you were upset, and then you were in trouble, because you didn't know what to do next. But if your goal all along had been behavior and activity over which you had control, you had no problem at all. The first negotiation was now followed by a second negotiation. Back to work! Big deal.

Beware Unworthy Goals

Setting unmanageable goals, those that are beyond your control, is one common mistake. Wasting time and energy on manageable but insufficient or unworthy goals is another. To make my point here, I draw a distinction between what I call *payside* and *nonpayside* activities. I apologize for the jargon and the mercenary tone, but the distinction is important, and I haven't figured out a better way to describe it. Payside activity is everything directly related to the negotiation, from setting valid appointments and meetings to making the final presentation. Nonpayside activity is stuff you have to do that isn't directly on the track of the negotiation. Filling out expense forms, for example, and other sorts of bureaucratic paperwork are the lowest form of nonpayside activity. In any event, I think you get the picture. For the salesperson, getting appointments with truly qualified prospects is a payside activity, while getting appointments with individuals or companies merely for the sake of fulfilling some mandatory quota is *not* a payside activity.

You do have to spend time and energy on nonpayside activities in order to get to payside, but, obviously, you want to keep the nonpayside to the minimum. A downfall of some gladhanding negotiators is to wine and dine potential customers, stop by their offices to shoot the breeze, play golf, send gifts, and so on—all nonpayside activities—while never making the move to get down to serious negotiating. This is pretty common, actually, in the corporate world, as well as in the more one-on-one professions, such as straight sales. These folks either don't know the difference between payside and nonpayside, or, more likely, they do know the difference very well and are kidding themselves and using all this nonpayside wining and dining to avoid what they know will be a difficult negotiation. With nonpayside activity, there's no immediate gain, but neither is there immediate *risk,* and this is tempting to us.

Payside activity does have potential reward, but it also holds risk, and it's hard work. This can thwart us—but we must not let it. On the day that I write these words, I have a meeting that could, in the future, lead to a serious $20 million negotiation. I'm going gladly, but I don't kid myself; it's nonpayside activity, and I'd set it aside in a moment for a payside activity on a negotiation worth only $1 million. One of the characteristics of really successful negotiators is how swiftly and efficiently they shift from nonpayside activity to payside activity.

There is great risk in believing, as per conventional wisdom, that certain activity is payside, when actually it's not. I'm thinking specifically of begging for an appointment—an extremely common error in all fields of business, as I've mentioned. I have seen salespeople almost ruined by this kind of nonpayside *dreaming*. A worthwhile appointment with a potential supplier or customer is definitely payside activity. An appointment rustled up out of the phone book to meet some kind of quota is definitely nonpayside and a horrible instance of self-deception. This appointment will fail, and so will the next one like it, and pretty soon, no matter how strong you are, your self-image will suffer and you'll really be in trouble. I mentioned in chapter 1 the salutary discipline imposed by cold calling, and this is true, but it is nonpayside activity. Be sure you understand this. Be sure you don't cold-call or do the equivalent if you have a legitimate payside activity waiting.

When we have the habit of setting as a goal *only* activity that we can accomplish and that is genuinely productive, we've taken the first step to getting some real work done. Rather than succeeding or not succeeding almost by accident in the service of some goal that's really beyond our control, we've taken the first step to taking responsibility for our actions and to end what is, really, self-deception (and probably companywide deception).

This may sound harsh, but it's the truth. It's too easy to sell or not sell fifty widgets this week, or to sign or fail to sign the contract with your supplier. It's much more difficult to behave and act at all times in a disciplined, systematic way. But this is what you must do in order to achieve what you're capable of.

A Daily Track Helps You Monitor Your Work

One of the most challenging skills to learn must be flying the ultrasophisticated military jet fighters. The training is rigorous, to say the least. This is a completely new environment for a young man or woman just out of college. The oxygen mask and parachute alone are restrictive enough to make you want to vomit. Sitting in a cockpit so small and with straps so tight you can barely move is also stifling. Flying at speeds of seven hundred miles per hour requires quick, effective decision making, to say the least again. There is no doubt that death can be instantaneous if the wrong decisions are made, so it is a gross understatement to say the young pilot faces a tremendous challenge. So how does the military, in twelve short months, turn this college graduate into a superb pilot? How does this pilot build the activity and behavior habits necessary to fulfill the goals?

Well, when this young man or woman checks into pilot training, one of the first items issued is the daily training folder. That record is carried at all times and reviewed by the instructor (coach) and the flight leader. It will be reviewed two or three times a day, with constant emphasis on reward for success and focused hard work on the failures. Under the circumstances, good habits are formed very quickly. The training folder will be a lasting document that will grow as the young pilot's career grows.

When the career is over, that training folder will become a historical document and part of this pilot's permanent military record.

Now I'm going to scare some of you with the answer to the following question: How do you, as a student of negotiation, turn newly learned activity and behavior into habit? You, too, should keep a daily record and use it to identify strengths and weaknesses. Though this is not a book about psychology, my system does ask the negotiator to study human nature, and it *requires* that the serious negotiator do so. You must understand and engage the adversary as a psychological being—an approach implicit throughout the previous discussion—and you must engage yourself in the same way. This daily habit of analyzing performance and correcting it is critical to success. It's something that many of us do at least some of the time—sometimes explicitly—and in my hands-on work as teacher and coach, I ask my students to make a commitment to daily, active self-examination and assessment, to monitor their behavior and emotions as they affect the negotiating process. Remember Vince Lombardi: "Winning isn't everything, but the will to prepare to win is everything."

For many people, this "daily track," as I call it, is a rigorous task. But I also know that keeping such a daily track would be as valuable in your negotiating work as anything else you might do. The critical assessment of daily actions and decision making pinpoints weaknesses, works with strengths, and develops self-esteem. This discipline makes you really stop to think how you're spending your time, how you're absorbing this material, how you're doing as a negotiator. As I've mentioned in the introduction, some theories of learning suggest that we need eight

hundred hours of practice to learn something new and complex.
Maybe that's high for some tasks, I don't know, but I do know
that we need lots of practice. The daily track helps us get it. I
urge you to make the commitment, and in the conclusion of this
book I'll explain how to set up your own daily track for establishing goals you can control, and then monitoring how well
you've done.

6

What Do You Say?

Fuels of the Camp System: Questions

HOW DO WE stop kidding ourselves, even lying to ourselves in negotiations? How do we preclude or correct misunderstandings? How do we identify the real issues and problems? How do we stop adversaries from hedging, fudging, and outright lying to us? How do we make deals that stick? How do we answer truthfully without destroying the feelings of someone else? We use the specific goals of behavior and action—goals we can control—that I call the "fuels of the system." These are the behavioral *habits* that allow us to peel the onion of the adversary's business situation and negotiating position and find out what's really going on over there.

The single most important fuel that you have, the most important behavioral goal and *habit* you can develop, is your ability to ask questions. The other fuels, which I introduce in the following chapter, support our questions. Perhaps this seems like kind of a small, maybe even quirky, subject for a chapter. In the first place, it's a short chapter, and in the second place it may be quirky, and it's certainly overlooked in every other book on negotiating I've ever seen, but the unwillingness or inability to ask good questions is a serious weakness in the field. They deserve their own chapter, believe me. If you master the art of questioning, your work as a negotiator will benefit enormously.

For many of us, the problem with questions is that we have been trained in our respective educational settings to be the smartest person in the room. How do we accomplish this? By *answering* questions, of course. Very few of us are trained to *ask* them, and even those whose professional work depends on this skill—I'm thinking of doctors and lawyers now—often don't do a very good job of it. Doctors can be so constrained by time and bureaucratic formulas, and so dependent on laboratory tests, that they forfeit one of their key diagnostic tools—asking good questions. I've had firsthand experience with this kind of medicine. I've also had the equivalent experience with lawyers, and I don't mean just in the courtroom, where the exchanges are tightly controlled by rules, but even in depositions, where the parties can take more liberties.

The doctor is trying to understand her patient's case, the lawyer is trying to find out as much as she can about the testifier's knowledge of the case, and the negotiator must try to see and understand her adversary's world. In any negotiation, where do we want to spend as much time as possible? In the adversary's world. If this wasn't your answer, that's okay, but it's the one I'll be looking for by the time we finish this book. Your mission and purpose is set in your adversary's world. Starting with M&P and going from there, you want to *inhabit* the adversary's world, because that is the world about which you need information, and that is the perspective from which the adversary makes decisions. He doesn't make decisions from *your* perspective, does he? Of course not. He makes them from his own perspective. Obviously. How do you find out about this perspective? How do you inhabit his world? By asking questions.

As I've already discussed, our decisions are, initially, 100 percent emotional. After we've made our emotion-based decision, we need time to get the clear picture, the clear vision with which to rationally judge that decision. Questions are the means by which the negotiator helps the adversary do this. The adversary's answers to our questions build the vision that he needs to make decisions.

No vision, no real decision: this is a rule of human nature.

The most pliable win-win folks won't buy a ten-cent trinket without some kind of vision of themselves or their children playing with this trinket. Right? If you have any doubt about this point, please take a moment to think about it. It's some vision in our mind's eye that leads us to buy *this* house, to plant *this* flower, to negotiate *this* deal. All of us make decisions based on the vision we have of the issue at hand. No vision, no decision. It's vital that you understand this point.

As a negotiator, questions are the fuels we use to lead the adversary to a vision that will serve as a catalyst for a decision. As much as possible, we want the negotiation to stay in our adversary's world. Questions do serve the further purpose of helping us control our own neediness and to be unokay—and this is a valuable purpose, I hope we all agree—but the vital purpose of questions is to allow us to move around in the adversary's world and see what they see and then lead them to a clear vision and decision as well.

The Power of *Correct* Questions

Asking questions is a science and an art. The science is in how you intellectually construct a question. The art is found in how you ask it: your tone of voice, your creative choice of words, your behavior and remarks before asking your question. So now we're going to get pretty technical, and we have to, because technique is everything here.

First, the "science." In the construction of our questions, we can start with a verb or with an interrogative. The verb-led question is just that, a question that begins with a verb.

"Is *this something you should do?*"
"Can *you do this?*"
"Will *you do this?*"
"Do *you need this?*"
"Do *you have five minutes to see me?*"

How many responses can such questions bring? Off the top, the majority of my new clients and workshop students say two. I wish it were so, but the correct answer is three.

"*Yes.*"
"*No.*"
"*Maybe.*"

I hope you remember the discussion of these three choices in chapter 3, "Start with No," and why, for a negotiator's purposes, "maybe" tells you nothing at all and "yes" is even worse. Only "no" tells you something real, gives you something to go on with your *next* question. With only one worthwhile answer out of the three, it follows that verb-led questions are often a waste of time. Therefore there are only two reasons to ask such a question: if you already know the answer (law students are taught just this rule), or if you're near the very end of the negotiation and you have to really bore in.

The answer to the verb-led question usually does not give you worthwhile information. That's one problem. Another problem is that such a question can often seem to the adversary as if you're driving for a "yes." "Can you do this?" is a perfect example. This question seems to the adversary to be calculated to take away the right to answer "no." It seems subtly manipulative, and usually it *is* subtly manipulative. Most people don't really want to say "no" in the first place, as we've discussed, so if your question makes it even harder for them to do so, you have created an uncomfortable, defensive adversary, and this does you no good at all.

Questions are so, so subtle. Consider the difference between the following choices:

"Is this what you really want?"
"Isn't this what you really want?"

Both are verb led, and therefore dubious, but the inclusion of the word "not" makes the second question a really terrible one, because of the insinuated "rush to close." Remember, "No Closing." Sooner or later in the negotiation, the attempt will backfire.

"Can you say yes to this?"

This is another terrible verb-led question. *Never* frame a question that seems to the adversary to be taking away the right to say "no."

"Is there any reason you wouldn't say yes to this?"

Even worse, if that's possible. *Never* frame a question that appears to your adversary as an attempt to trick. Everyone reading this book would flinch when hearing that question, and yet they do hear that question, or the equivalent, all too often from inexperienced negotiators.

This point must be clear: Framing any question is very tricky and very important. You can blow a solid one-hour presentation in less than one minute with an ill-chosen, one-sentence question such as "Is there any reason you wouldn't say yes to this?" But it happens every second of the day, somewhere, because the ill-trained negotiator has been led to believe that he's *supposed* to ask such a question in order to push things along quickly.

But what if I were to ask this question:

"What would you like me to do?"

Well, this simple question is of a different sort altogether. This question spawns some interesting dynamics. Mainly, it is a very comforting question to hear. It demonstrates that you, the negotiator who has asked this question, has no needs at the table. You have opened an area for negotiation and shown no fear. You are making no assumptions. The adversary feels okay, because you are at her service. You are certainly not closing, attempting to confuse, or any of that negative stuff. Hearing this question, the adversary on the other side of the table has no reason to fear you.

Just as important, this open-ended question does not have a quick answer. It *cannot* be answered with yes, no, or maybe. The necessarily more extended answer will have—well, may have—some information, or some emotion, or some telltale waffling, or some insight. It should have *something* you can work with, because, as we know, people have a weakness for talking.

Who has control in a conversation, the guy listening or the guy talking? The listener, of course. If you want to maintain maximum control and leverage—and you do, of course—let your adversary do the talking. With a question such as "What would you like me to do?" you invite the adversary to indulge this weakness. Moreover, her answer allows you to enter her world and her vision.

Likewise, when I ask, "How are you?" whose world am I entering? Whose world am I entering when I ask, "Now why did you invite me to this meeting?" Whose world when I ask, "What's the biggest challenge your company faces?"

Have you noticed the main difference between these good questions and any of the previous bad questions? The good ones are led by an *interrogative*, not by a verb. "Who," "what," "when," "where," "why," "how," and "which": These are the famous interrogatives we all learned about in elementary school, I guess. They begin the safe, effective questions in a negotiation. They will move the negotiation forward without the pitfalls of verb-led questions. You have to be diligent and careful with all questions—with every word you utter—but the verb-led questions are almost all downside, while these interrogative-led questions are a key means of discovery. They elicit details. They ensure thoroughness. They help the adversary, as well as us, see what hasn't been seen and understood before.

I'm sure you didn't register—there's no reason you should have—that the first sentence of my introduction was an interrogative-led question: *How often over the past couple of decades have we read or heard the phrase "win-win"?* My strategy was simple. In order to open your mind to my contrarian approach, I thought I needed to challenge immediately, right in the first paragraph, the reigning paradigm in negotiation, which is win-win. But in order to do this I had to create in your mind a vision of its omnipresence in our culture. What better way to do this than with a question led by an interrogative?

It's Hard to Go Wrong with Interrogative-Led Questions

Many readers have probably participated in role-playing games in workshops. They're pretty much a staple in the business world, and they really can be useful, so let's try one now. Close your eyes. Relax. Let your muscles go limp. You are allowed to be anywhere you would like to be. You may be with anyone you choose, doing anything you would like to do. Okay, let's play. *Where* are you? *Whom* are you with? *What* are you doing? Maybe you're somewhere in the tropics with a beach in the foreground, or maybe you're skiing down a mountain with a chalet and a hot toddy in the background. In any case, your ability to envision the scene will have a direct effect on your ability to help others gain a clear picture of what you would like them to see. This was *your* picture, *your* world that I was finding out about through the use of interrogatives. In just this way the interrogative-led question in a negotiation helps you to turn on your adversary's picture tube. The interrogative-led question helps you help the adversary to turn on their own vision and to paint clear pictures, so that both sides have the *same* picture. It gives you the power to see what they see, and you need to. Otherwise, there will be no progress in this negotiation.

Here is a set of verb-led questions juxtaposed with an equivalent interrogative-led question on the same subject. In every case, which is the better question?

"Is this the biggest issue we face?" versus *"What is the biggest issue we face?"*

"Is this proposal tight enough for you?" versus *"How can I tighten this proposal?"*

"Can we work on delivery dates tomorrow?" versus *"When can we work on delivery dates?"* or *"How important are delivery dates?"*

"Do you think we should bring Mary into the loop now?" versus *"Where does Mary fit in?"* or *"When should we bring Mary into the loop?"*

"Is there anything else you need?" versus *"What else do you need?"*

"Do you like what you see?" versus *"What are your thoughts?"*

"Is it too expensive?" versus *"What price would you pay?"*

"Does it fit into your needs?" versus *"How do you see it?* or *"Where would you use it?"*

This rule about interrogative-led questions is not rocket science. Negotiators have been taught for decades to ask open-ended questions, and interrogative-led questions are simply one type of open-ended questions. I emphasize the interrogative-led idea rather than the open-ended idea because I've found that the former rule is easier to understand and to follow in the heat of a negotiation. Interrogative-led questions can be closed, of course—"What time is it?" is an example—but, generally speaking, the negotiator who frames interrogative-led questions is on the right track.

You might be thinking, *Well, okay, but this discussion is too simple and stagy, it doesn't sound very real world to me; does it really apply in the world of big-time negotiating?* This is a fair question. Some of my examples have been a little stagy, for the sake of

simplicity and clarity. But now let me list in order the sequence
of questions asked in a phone call by a client working for a large
corporation. His adversary worked for an even larger corporation. This was one of hundreds of such conversations—in person, on the phone, and by e-mail—during the course of a long
negotiation. The subject here is intentionally unclear, but for
our purposes the subject doesn't matter. Here are the questions:

"Why did your previous boss want you to get with me?"
"Why were we added?"
"Who was your old boss?"
"How did that affect us?"
"Where are we at in the process?"
"What happened?"
"Where will you be?"
"Like what?"
"How can I help you succeed?"
"Who will pull all these factions together within [unnamed
    corporation]?"
"How should I work with [unnamed]?"
"How should I proceed?"
"What are [unnamed company's] plans at the facility in [unnamed
    American city]?"
"What are the plans for the [unnamed project]?"
"What influence does [unnamed project] have in all this?"
"How should I proceed?"
"Why are you asking?"
"Who are they?"

I don't claim that I picked this conversation completely
at random, but I assure you that it's quite typical. My clients
really do live and die—mostly live, mostly thrive—by asking

interrogative-led questions. One client was recently brought into a negotiation with a large multinational to be the competitive vendor for a primary vendor. We understood that this was the dynamic and accepted it, and we also knew that the primary vendor would have a powerful constituency within the multinational's own middle management, because some such liaison is almost a given. Such a situation must be addressed up front by any negotiator. We therefore framed the following question to ask at the highest possible level (CEO to senior vice president, specifically): *"How* do we keep our efforts from being sabotaged by someone within your company who's responsible for the competitor's success?" In this instance, the answer was the senior vice president's instruction to the in-house spear carrier for the primary vendor to be certain that my *client's* efforts came to fruition. The man's annual bonus now depended on it.

Think back a little bit more about mission and purpose. Remember the "features and benefits" to your adversary that we want to be part of our mission and purpose? Such features and benefits can also be a part of your questions. The words that describe a feature or a benefit can be placed in the question to help the adversary see a problem. Say our rough-and-ready mission and purpose for this negotiation is "To have Humongous, Inc., see and decide that having our technology will meet all their needs now and in the future." One good interrogative-led question to fit into an early discussion might be *"How* can you stay competitive without this technology?"

Notice the vital difference between that question and *"Can* you stay competitive without this technology?" The point of both questions is to lead the adversary to see that they *cannot* stay competitive otherwise, but the question led by the verb "can" sounds faintly accusatory and might put the adversary

on the defensive, while the question led by the interrogative
"how" is softer, less threatening, and more inviting of a straightforward, worthwhile answer. Once again, the advantage goes to
the interrogative-led question.

Let's return to the story in chapter 2 about Network, Inc., the
company that needed to renegotiate the contract for its machines, because each one was being sold at a loss. Say our mission and purpose for this negotiation is "To help [the other
company's] management at the very highest level see our company as a new and revitalized organization that is going to
change its effectiveness . . ." One good interrogative-led question to fit into an early discussion might be "How will you measure us from this point forward?"

Let's return to the infamous negotiation involving the baseball
umpires, which we talked about in chapter 4. Say their mission
and purpose is, as I've already suggested, "to get the players, the
fans, and the lords of the game to see and decide that the umpires provide the highest level of expertise in calling balls and
strikes and plays at the bases while remaining invisible on the
field." One good interrogative-led question to fit into an early
discussion might be "How long does it take to develop a great
umpire?" Another might be "How many bad calls does it take to
really hurt a baseball game?"

I urge you to play these hypothetical games, because the
power of the simple interrogative-led question is just amazing.
I've had clients for whom this understanding was a eureka moment that turned around their whole careers as negotiators.
Their appreciation of the difference between these disarming
questions and all others seemed to loosen them up in a fundamental way. Their own neediness came under control. They
now understood that a successful negotiation really does take

place in the adversary's world, not in their own. They suddenly understood the necessity of creating vision in the adversary.

No vision, no decision? Of course. And now I add, no interrogative-led questions, no vision, no decision.

Keep It Simple

Keep your questions short. Anytime a question has more than, say, nine or ten words you risk complication. You may think that a lengthy compound question sounds impressive, but you're not in the business of sounding impressive, remember. Such a question serves only to kill vision and confuse your adversary. Remember when I said that if our own mission and purpose is too cloudy, we make it difficult for our adversary to make a decision? The same thing goes with questions.

Another key is to ask *one question at a time.* Simple question by simple question, answer by answer, you will help your adversary build his own picture of the issue. But often we don't do this. A negotiation is a very emotional arena, of course, and we get impatient and load one question on top of another, asking five or six in a row, barely pausing to take a breath, much less letting the adversary answer. Instead, you must take each question slow and easy and listen to each answer, because that answer is the clue for framing the next question.

"When is your ideal delivery date?"
"How critical is this November date for you?"
"I'm not sure I understand. Why is November so important?"
"Oh, when did that problem on the production line show up?"

Interesting news! And it happens all the time, because mixed in with everything else in the answers to good questions will be some spilled beans. (I discuss this phenomenon at length in chapter 8.)

There seems to be a human impulse to help people answer our questions. We start off with a good interrogative-led question but then answer it *for* the adversary, or at the least throw out possible answers. I ask, "What is the biggest challenge you face?" and before you have a chance to answer I add, "Is it the national economy or your local labor problems?" One mistake on top of another: We answered the question for our adversary and in doing so our interrogative-led question turned into a verb-led question. All we accomplish with this intervention is to impede the process by which the adversary creates a vision for himself and for us regarding his company's greatest challenge.

I've mentioned the clients for whom their sudden understanding of the power of interrogative-led questions was a eureka moment. For many others, the art of asking questions has become a standing challenge. They really get into it. They understand that asking great questions is an art, a science, and a necessary skill for succeeding at the highest level.

7

How Do You Say It?

More Fuels of the Camp System

ASKING GOOD QUESTIONS is the highest octane fuel we have. They are a key behavioral goal. Of the five other behavioral goals that I call the fuels of the system, four work in direct support of our questions. They help us control *what* we say. They help us use our words to our advantage. I call these four fuels nurturing, reversing, connecting, and 3+. The fifth fuel, unrelated to questions, is the strip line.

There are some quirky names in that list, but that's okay. Much of the behavior they require is contrarian to conventional win-win wisdom. It is this contrarian and unexpected behavior that allows us to transcend the average and gives us a great advantage.

Nurturing

We all know what the word means. "Nurturing" means to feed emotionally, to provide moral training, to foster the mind with good and understanding and appreciative thoughts. Who brings good nurturing thoughts and memories to your mind? Maybe it was your grandmother who always had a kind word, or your mom or dad when she or he tucked you in at night, or others who put you at ease by the way in which they talked to you. Maybe it was a warm, soft conversation, or a conversation that was heavy with respect. What you had to say was important to this individual, and she or he wanted to listen. Just to be *listened to* can bring good thoughts to mind.

In a negotiation, nurturing will keep the negotiation going through thick and thin. Your ability to nurture will be the key to bringing the negotiation back to the table after a breakdown. Your ability to nurture your adversary, to put him or her at ease, is the key to assuring her that you are listening and that you value what she has to say. Nurturing is also just another way to allow your adversary to feel okay.

Nurturing should be part of your body language. When you're seated, refrain from a sudden forward movement. Lean back. Relax your neck, face, and hands. If you're standing, lean against the wall, lower your posture. No one is going to deal effectively with you if you're towering over them. This is common sense, and even an average negotiator would pretty much adhere to this principle. But a lot of average negotiators give out the wrong signals in less obvious ways. They lean forward and jerk their arms and smack the table. The truly comfortable, trained negotiator takes it easy. When in doubt, slow your cadence of speech, lower your voice. As the old saying goes, laughter often is the best medicine, especially laughter directed at ourselves. Laughter is a way to nurture everyone in the room—including ourselves. Now, none of this is contrarian at all. Granted, you won't find a section about nurturing in most negotiation books, but that's just because those authors are trying to impress you with their arcane academic theories and charts and graphs. They wouldn't disagree with me on this point; they just *incorrectly* believe it's not hotshot material.

The way you phrase questions and statements can be either nurturing or almost the opposite. Let's revisit some of the questions from the discussion so far and find the nurturing in them. "Hey, how's it going?" This is nurturing. "That's a good question." This is nurturing. "Boy, you look grim." Not quite so nurturing unless you're teasing a good friend. "That question does nothing for me." Not quite so nurturing.

Even more important than what you say for nurturing purposes is *how* you say it. Think of the sentence "Is this what you really want?" These six words can cut either way. If I say them abruptly and abrasively, they're the opposite of nurturing. But if I ask the question quietly and with concern, even though it's a verb-led question, it's very nurturing. I see nothing wrong with taking a minute right now to put this book down and ask that question aloud in a number of ways, including "IS THIS WHAT YOU REALLY WANT?!" and, softly, "Is this what you *really* want?" You'll immediately see the differences on the nurturing scale. Delivery is everything. We all know this, but too often we forget it.

Please don't misunderstand me. I'm not into touchy-feely negotiations. Nurturing must not be confused with being easy and soft. Nurturing does not signal arbitrary compromise. It does not mean "saving the adversary" from a tough decision. Nurturing is simply a psychological move that allows just a little stress to be released at the right moment. One of the toughest men of the twentieth century was Sir Winston Churchill, but if you study his writings and listen to recordings of his speeches you will discover both his bulldog toughness *and* his nurturing moves. If you listen to his speeches on tape, you will hear his naturally nurturing voice. Likewise, Joe Lieberman, vice presidential candidate for the Democratic Party in 2000, became known for his naturally nurturing voice and demeanor. He could say almost anything and get away with it. Think of a psychologist trying to pry out your deepest, darkest secrets. Is she going to do so with a harsh, challenging voice, or with a calm, gentle voice?

Nurturing requires the delicate touch. Nurturing may be just the one right word, or facial expression, or gesture. How you nurture will require great practice, insight, and reflection. When the going gets tough in a negotiation, your biggest challenge will be your ability to nurture your adversary in spite of everything else going on. I should put that in boldface capital letters—but I won't, because that wouldn't be very nurturing, would it?

Reversing

This is a behavior that you must hone to perfection for successful negotiations. The reverse is the behavioral tactic that answers a question with a question, the answer to which will do you some good. When your adversary asks you a question, you do have to say something, but not in the way in which you were trained in school.

"How are you?"
"Great. How are you?*"*

That's a reverse, isn't it? And effective. But more often than not, for a variety of reasons, untrained negotiators aren't alert for the opportunity to answer questions by asking questions. Maybe they're too busy talking up themselves and divulging information. Many times they assume that they already know the answer. Or they don't understand the difference between verb-led and interrogative-led questions, and they're tired of hearing "no" in response to incorrect verb-led questions. Meanwhile, the trained negotiator looks for every opportunity to answer a question with a question.

Vital point: The reverse should be preceded by a short *nurturing* statement, because you don't want to sound like a district attorney during cross-examination. Without the nurturing tidbit, the reverse will do you little good, but if you have any doubt that the *nurturing* reverse works, try it the next time you're talking with someone at the proverbial watercooler. We human beings are seduced by it every time.

"Jim, what will this option do for me?"
"That's a good question, Dick. Before we get into that, what's the biggest challenge you're facing in this area?"

Nurture, reverse:

"That was certainly well thought out. By the way, what are your cost constraints?"
"We definitely have to talk about that, but before we go there . . ."
"Interesting. Really interesting. How soon will you be up against a deadline here?"
"That's something I hadn't thought of. When could you deliver?"

*"Hmmm. What am I missing here? What else can you tell me
about that?"*

My son Brian now plays college football for a major program.
He was not the high school recruit I mentioned in chapter 3, but
when Brian was being recruited a couple of years ago, he was
asked by the dean of students with arguably the most prestigious
and respected football program in the country, "What do you
think would be the most challenging part of playing football for
this school?" Brian's answer was rather long, but it was a great
reverse: "Gee, that's a great question. I'd like to toss it back at
you because I've got so many things going through my mind. I'd
like your help in understanding how you really see it, because
you've got so much experience in this. What are the things I
should really be aware of?" Most potential recruits who came
through this dean's office were making a required stop and could
not have cared less about anything the man had to say. But this
Camp-trained recruit—my son—had let the dean know that he
wasn't a cocky, self-aggrandizing kid who thought he had all the
answers. (There are a lot of these kids around, you know, and
quite a few such adults as well.) The recruit also allowed the
dean to be the most okay person in the room—always a plus.
The dean was delighted to have a kid who actually seemed to respect his opinion, and he was a great source of insight into the
way the campus worked and the unusual pressures on football
players, since it is such a high-profile program. When we drove
through the gates at the end of the visit, Brian said, "I don't
want to go to school in a museum."

On another campus, Brian was interviewing with the highly
respected football coach. (I apologize for using two such examples in a row, but both speak to the subject of reversing, and the

fact that each was carried out by an eighteen-year-old high school student demonstrates that the behavioral goal of reversing is readily available to all of us.) This coach was talking to Brian about his size, which is large, and then he asked Brian how flexible he was. Brian quickly reversed and said, "In my high school, we work pretty hard with weights, Coach. How much emphasis do you put on weight lifting in your program?" The coach told my son that he didn't really believe in a lot of weight training for quarterbacks, Brian's position at the time. The coach was concerned that the size and strength of today's quarterbacks was limiting their flexibility. My son hadn't studied the physiology of exercise, but he knew that the coach's concern was grounded in exercise theories of twenty years ago and almost falls into the category of myth today. In the last three or four years, hasn't Tiger Woods totally destroyed old-time myths about how strength exercises are bad for the "flexibility sports"? And look at the baseball players, even the pitchers. So there is no room in modern athletics for that coach's outmoded and incorrect thinking, and my son's simple reverse gave him all the information he needed about that program. The coach's answer was one of the reasons Brian didn't go to that particular school.

In any negotiation, the reverse assures that you're dealing with an important question *for you,* thereby allowing you to gather more insight and information. Your job is to get information from the adversary by asking questions, not to provide information by answering questions. Reversing is nothing more than the lawyer's standard technique of clarification. Questions and reversing help us get into the world of the adversary. They are the way we create vision. Without reversing and asking questions, we'll get nowhere.

Sometimes you may feel you *absolutely* have to give some kind of answer. In this case, give a no-risk answer. If your adversary asks your opinion about a given matter, what she's really after is your agreement. Don't give it to her.

"Well, Mary, I know how you feel and I really respect your opinion, but to tell you the truth, I haven't had time to solidify my opinion. You may be right. I'm sort of going both ways. But your opinion is always in the back of my mind."

You haven't given up any information, and you have ever so subtly made your adversary think you're supporting her position without actually doing so.

"How much does it cost?"
"A lot."
"How long have you guys been working on this?"
"It seems like forever!"

You're satisfying the necessity of answering, but the information you're giving is, for all intents and purposes, not worth much. Most of the time, however, your adversary will not recognize this, will accept the answer, and will be open to a good question from you.

Connecting

As I've said in several contexts, we have a tendency to want to save our adversary, to be liked. This instinct can impel us into these three common negotiating errors, which I have derived from what every attorney tells his client before a deposition or testimony: never answer an unasked question; don't interpret a statement as a question; and never reply to random statements.

"I don't like what I see, Jim."

When we hear this, many of us will feel an urge to reply in some way, to try to set things right.

"Well, Damon, this isn't written in concrete."

No! The best way to deal with the leading unasked question or the provocative remark is to use it as a basis for prying out more information. How? By employing what I call a *connector.* To respond is average negotiating behavior; to *connect* is contrarian negotiating behavior, and much more effective. Think about the psychiatrist, whose job is to help the client understand his problems and then deal with them. Here's one possible exchange:

> *"Doctor, you're not helping me."*
> *"I think I am helping you."*
> *"No, you're not helping me at all."*
> *"Of course I'm helping you."*
> *"If you're helping me so much, then why do I feel so bad?"*
> *"Well, you feel bad because you're not committed."*
> *"I am committed, you're just not a very good shrink."*

The patient is correct. This is not a good shrink. Now let's see how the nurturing connector might have improved the exchange.

> *"Doctor, you're not helping me at all."*
> *"Help me understand."*
> *"Well, I just don't feel as though I am making any progress."*
> *"Annnnnd?"*

"I'm having trouble doing the exercises you told me to do."
"I see. What's the most difficult problem you are having with the exercises?"

That little word "and," when asked as a question, is an excellent connector.

"I don't like what I see, Jim."
"Aannnnnnnnd?" [This is drawn out, accompanied by a shrug. The adversary now has to fill in the picture for Jim.]
"I can't get too excited about this until I see your competition."

Fine. You've learned something.

In effect, the connection is another type of reverse. Your adversary's floating remark, gauged to get some kind of reaction from you, is turned around with the intent of getting some kind of useful information from him.

"Wow. This is pretty much out of nowhere."
"Which means . . . ?" [Accompanied by a shrug.]
"This isn't going to happen unless you lose a zero."

Fine again. You've learned something.

Profound, silent concern on your part can also serve as a connector. People don't like silence. It's the void that our nature abhors. Your adversary will rush to fill in the blank.

"Wow. This is pretty much out of nowhere."
Silence.
"This isn't going to happen unless you can deliver next month."

Now you're really getting somewhere. The connector, like the reverse, has helped get us to the real issue.

"I don't like your attitude."
"How can I help you?"
"Your price is too high."

This is real progress. Your attitude was never the problem.

Again, these little dialogues are on the stagy side, I admit, but they're not all that stagy. In somewhat extended form, they happen every day. The trained negotiator *practices* every day.

3+

The fuel "3+" (pronounced "three plus") is simple and important. What is it? Nothing more than the ability to remain with a question until it is answered at least three times, or to repeat a statement at least three times. This is not an original idea. Anyone who's ever taken a speech class knows the old rule: Tell them what you're going to tell them, tell them, tell them what you told them. One, two, *three* times. I first heard the equivalent rule many, many years ago from a salesman friend and quickly learned that this was good advice. I've added the "+" because I've found that three times often isn't enough. So I coach 3+ times. The more critical the negotiation, the more times over a longer period of time you may need to reiterate the agreed-upon point. In practice, it's difficult to overdo the 3+. Almost impossible.

In the conference call that started the Network, Inc., renegotiation regarding the contract that was losing $100,000 per machine shipped, the president of Network actually informed his adversaries that he would repeat what he had to say about the problem three times, because it was so serious he wanted to make sure it was clear and understood by each and every one of them. I don't usually coach that you literally announce that you will use 3+, but it was appropriate to do so in this negotiation.

Of course you must nurture or reverse with 3+. You have to make certain that the agreement you're hearing from the adversary on this particular is truly agreement. As always, you're extremely suspicious of "yes." Most of all, you cannot sound *needy* to nail down this point of agreement. The 3+ technique cannot seem to the adversary like pressure in any way; it cannot *be* pressure in any way. When you use 3+, you always have to leave the option for the adversary to change his mind. You are *not* rushing to close three times. Just the opposite, of course: You're asking for "no" three times. That's the way to think about it.

How many times have you tried to make a decision and had thoughts like this run through your mind?

"I'm going to do it."
"No, I'm not."
"Yeah, I think I am."
"I hate it. I'm not going to do it."

Whether we use 3+ or 20+, we always give the adversaries the opportunity to go through this process in their own minds. The 3+ technique goes hand in hand with "never close." The whole point of 3+ is to give the adversary multiple opportunities to look at their decision—to verify it, to justify it, or to change it. We give the adversary every chance to think through the situation, look at it from different perspectives, and see for themselves how their thinking changes. The adversary doesn't always see what they should see, and using the 3+ technique helps them get a good picture. No vision, no decision.

The Strip Line

I introduce the strip line, the last of the fuels of the system, with the analogy of the pendulum swinging back and forth, back and forth, back and forth. That's what a negotiation can be like. Initially, the pendulum is stationary. Emotions are calm, neither positive nor negative. Then something happens, someone says something, and this force pushes the pendulum into the negative, say. Then some factor halts the movement into the negative and pulls the pendulum all the way past neutral and toward the positive. All these back-and-forth emotional swings can be catastrophic to the negotiation, especially if they're big and dramatic. The task of the good negotiator is to keep the pendulum as close as possible to a calm, stationary mode. The big negative swings don't do anyone any good in the long run, and neither do the big *positive* swings.

Let's take a straight sales situation, although the picture works just as well for any negotiation of any kind. If you, the salesperson, allow the potential customer to swing too hard into the positive mode, what happens when the *inevitable* second thoughts and doubts set in? The pendulum that was high in the positive mode swings down with so much momentum it carries all the way through neutral and into the hard *negative* mode. Now what do you do? This may be a position from which you never recover. Of course, the eternal optimist says, well, the next change of emotion will carry it from deep in the negative back to high in the positive. Okay, fine. But then what? You see? These big swings are a vicious cycle, so to speak, and they're almost impossible to control. But you must maintain control. So what's the solution? It's simple (in theory): Avoid both the *strongly* negative and the *strongly* positive by staying in the calm *neutral* range, which is where we find the deals that stick. This is totally contrarian negotiating. *You mean we don't want the adversary to get all excited about this deal?* No, we don't, because the excitement won't last; those inevitable second thoughts will come along sooner or later.

How do we stay in the neutral range and keep all the emotions under control during a negotiation? We use the strip line, a reference to a technique in bonefishing (and other types of fishing as well) in which you feed line to the fish when it first takes the bait, rather than set the hook. This is the only way to catch bonefish, which take off at incredible speeds the moment they're hooked. With bonefish, setting the hook immediately just rips it right out. By stripping line, you avoid putting on too much pressure.

Likewise in a negotiation: by stripping line you take the pressure off the adversary. It is an extremely effective tool, and it's a lot of fun for me to see the initial doubt about the strip line on the part of my clients turn into enthusiastic endorsement, as they see how effective it is. Sometimes they get so excited I have to use strip line to draw them back a little! It's not a panacea, just a darned good tool.

Now that I've introduced this idea of releasing pressure, you can see that 3+ is also a way to release pressure. So is giving the adversary the right to say "no." So is allowing the adversary to be okay. So is "No Closing." When used effectively, the strip line, like those other behavioral goals, will allow your adversary the opportunity to validate information and decisions that have gone before.

The Negative Strip Line

The strip line comes in different types to be used in different situations. The first type I'll examine is the *negative* strip line, which I'll illustrate first with the movie *Legal Eagles,* in which that great actor Robert Redford plays an experienced assistant district attorney who has just been fired for complicated reasons. For other complicated reasons, Redford joins Debra Winger, a small-time defense attorney, in her advocacy on behalf of the Daryl Hannah character, a beautiful young woman accused of killing her lover. This is a dream case for the scandal sheets and way over Winger's inexperienced head. The prosecution has a murder weapon, a motive, and an eyewitness who puts the defendant at the scene. It's apparent from the reaction to the prosecution's opening statement that the jury and the press have already found Redford's new client guilty.

This is an open–and–shut case. Picture a packed courtroom and a circuslike atmosphere as the district attorney finishes his powerful introduction. How should Redford proceed? How could he possibly shift the pendulum even a little away from the powerfully negative and toward the neutral? He begins his opening remarks in a normal fashion: "Ladies and gentlemen, Chelsea Deardon did not kill Victor Taft. The prosecution has suggested a possible motive, but one based entirely on hearsay, conjecture, and circumstantial evidence, evidence that on the surface would appear to have some substance, but upon closer examination will prove to have no relevance whatsoever to this case." Okay, a decent start, but the camera tells us that Redford's remarks are falling on deaf ears in the jury box. He knows this as well, of course. And here comes the hard, negative strip line. Redford stops suddenly, looks into the jury's eyes, tilts his head in that winning way of his, and says, "You're not buying this, are you? You're not listening to a word I'm saying. Really. Right?" Pregnant pause. "Guess what? I don't blame you. After listening to the prosecution's evidence, even *I'm* convinced my client murdered Victor Taft. After all, if I'd walked into the room and found Victor Taft dead on the floor and Chelsea Deardon's fingerprints all over the weapon that killed him, there isn't much in the world that wouldn't convince me she was guilty. Look, let's just save ourselves a lot of time here. . . . Who thinks Chelsea Deardon is guilty?" When Redford asks for a show of hands on this question, the prosecution objects. The judge grumbles.

Redford continues, "Come on. I've got my hand raised. I believe that my client murdered Victor Taft in cold blood. Who agrees with me? Come on!" More objections, more grumbles. "Let's save the state of New York a lot of time and money and move directly to sentencing." Redford has gone so negative even his cocounsel, who didn't know what was coming, is having her doubts. The defendant is beside herself. With the courtroom now in chaos, the judge calling for order, reporters racing for the phones, Redford finds himself near the jury box, where one respectable-looking, middle-aged woman (played by the actress Liz Sheridan, who later in her career played Jerry Seinfeld's mother on his TV series, by the way) asks softly, "Isn't she entitled to a fair trial?" Redford replies instantly, "Oh, let's give her a fair trial and *then* convict her."

By now the judge has had enough, disqualifies the jury, and threatens Redford with contempt. Redford begs the judge's indulgence. He says he's perfectly happy with this jury and has faith in them, even though they believe his client is guilty. The prosecutor expresses his satisfaction with this jury, and the judge relents.

Brilliant negotiating by Redford. With the emotional pendulum set solidly in the negative area in the beginning, he used his hard, negative strip line—"You're not buying this, are you?"—to insinuate himself right into the *heart* of that negative emotion. What was he trying to accomplish? Stabilization, that's all. He wanted to wake up the jury to their bias and plant a second thought. By joining their decision of "no," he had enticed them into shifting into the intellectual mode, if only for a moment. Remember that the value of the word "no" is that it is, unlike "maybe," a real decision, and as a decision it has to be intellectually validated by the adversary—by the jury, in this particular negotiation. Redford has their full attention now. They were still negative, but at least they were thinking. Then he said, "You're not listening to a word I'm saying." That was another hard strip line that nudged the emotional pendulum just a little more toward neutral. Then came "Guess what? I don't blame you!"— another hard strip line.

How many negative strip lines are required in a given negotiation is always a judgment call, but a good rule of thumb is to continue until you see, or feel, evidence of significant movement by that pendulum. When Redford finally feels it with this jury, he subtly introduces the presumption of innocence: "So we all think she's guilty. Now what do we do? It's a dilemma, isn't it? It's an especially difficult problem because we've developed a legal concept in this country to protect ourselves, to protect our rights. It's called the presumption of innocence."

And you know that Darryl Hannah is soon found innocent— or, rather, the case against her is dismissed when the actual murderer is discovered. *Legal Eagles* is definitely not a great movie, but that was a great negative strip line by Robert Redford. Hats off.

Now, a real-life story: I recently switched cell phone companies because the spotty coverage I was experiencing was intolerable. I travel a lot and require as close to nationwide coverage as I can get, but the last straw with this company was the day I couldn't get through to San Francisco as I was driving up from San Jose. And it wasn't my phone unit, because I had invested in a high-end phone. When I got home I called the company to stop my service and gave the guy the reason I was switching to a competitor. What do you think he said? Here are his exact words:

"What do you mean? I was just in San Francisco and didn't have any problems. We have great coverage."

I don't know about your reaction to this statement, but in my book this guy was calling me a liar. Think of the other mistakes he made as well. He took away my right to say "no," he didn't allow me to feel okay, he didn't ask good questions to get a little more information, and he didn't strip line. (He did use an interrogative-led question, which just proves that you still have to use your head and your common sense when following the rule to ask interrogative-led questions. His wasn't a nurturing question, to say the least.) I was so strongly negative on this outfit, this guy could have offered me the world and I would have said no thank you, but what if he had used a strip line and said: "I'd probably switch companies too, if that happened to me. But before you do that, why don't you let me give you a free upgrade and check out our coverage for ten days?"

His negative strip line would have neutralized my harshly

negative emotional state. Who knows, he might have hooked me for at least another ten days, and he might have saved the situation. There is no better tool around than the *hard* negative strip line to neutralize a negative pendulum swing and get the situation into the neutral range. Try it sometime.

Find a good opportunity to say, "Wow, this is bad. I don't know if we can ever recover from this." Quite likely, your adversary will then *help* you recover. It's so much fun when this happens.

The Positive Strip Line

Now, the *positive* strip line is just that: a way to bring the adversary back toward a more neutral position from a position that's too positive—yes, *too* positive. The well-trained car salesman puts a slight damper on his customer's excitement over the black car by saying, "Black is a powerful color for a sports car, but it sure shows the dirt. It'll take work." This brings the positive adversary closer to neutral and at the same time urges him to validate his own enthusiasm for the color black—his *vision* of the color black. He replies, "Yeah, but if I buy this car, keeping it clean will be a pleasure."

Workshop students have said to me at this stage of my spiel, "You must be kidding." Hardly. In all honesty, I could not name one instance in which a positive strip line ever backfired. It just never backfires. To believe that it might is to misunderstand human nature and your purpose as a negotiator.

The lightest possible strip line is used to bring the adversary back toward neutral almost as the icing on the cake. It controls any neediness of your own, reinforces the adversary's right to say "no," lets the adversary be okay, and gets you deals that stick. Believing that the positive strip is dangerous reveals that you're stuck in a "rush to close" mode. Remember, everything hinges on your adversary's vision. You want to do everything you can to build that vision. The positive strip line does just that, as you will learn the minute you put this fuel into practice.

> *"Before you sign this deal, are you sure this is something you really want to do?"*
>
> *"Yes, I've thought about it a great deal and it makes perfect sense."*

Or:

> *"That's great, Joan. I appreciate your interest, but we still have a lot of challenges to work on."*

Nirvana

Right about now you may be thinking, *Wait a minute, Camp, in this chapter and the preceding one on the fuels of the Camp system, you've been introducing ways to obtain as* much *information from the adversary as possible while divulging as* little *information as possible. What happens when you run into an adversary who* also *knows the Jim Camp system?*

I wish it were so! Such a negotiation would proceed at a splendid pace. Both sides would be working from valid mission and purpose statements and with valid goals. Both parties would put their cards on the table at an early stage of the negotiation. Both sides would be quick to say "no" and then to explain why. We wouldn't have to engage in reversing and connecting in order to pry out information and answers. We wouldn't need strip line in order to keep everyone's emotions on an even keel. The fuels of the system are means to elicit information and to keep the negotiation moving smoothly. With two Camp-trained negotiators as adversaries, this smooth exchange is almost a given.

8

Quiet Your Mind, Create a Blank Slate

No Expectations, No Assumptions, No Talking

I N MY SYSTEM, "blank slate" is a verb. As negotiators, we actively blank slate in order to *create* a blank slate in our own minds, which then sits ready and waiting to receive any new information, new attitudes, new emotions, or new anything that our adversary wittingly or unwittingly beams our way. It is through blank slating that we learn what's really going on in this negotiation—what's really holding things up, what the adversary really *needs*.

Blank slate is a key behavioral goal that you will have to practice over and over and over. For successful negotiations, it must become a habit. And in order to blank slate you're probably going to have to *give up* some habits that you may think are beneficial but are hurting you in more ways than you can imagine. I've already pointed out some of the dangers of neediness. Another danger of neediness of any kind is that it interferes with blank slating. So does the fear of hearing "no" and the fear of failing. Obviously the tendency of some of us to "know it all" interferes with blank slating, because if we know it all, why bother to listen?

All of these negative behavioral activities that we've already discussed have to go out the window in the interests of blank slating. But once we do get the hang of blank slate, we become so focused and intense that we almost feel we're stepping out of our bodies, going to a corner of the room, and watching ourselves negotiate with the adversary. It's an exhilarating feeling.

Your ability to blank slate is directly related to your ability to rid yourself of expectations and assumptions, two very bad words in my system of negotiation. Real taboos. By nature, we humans are chock-full of expectations and assumptions. As a negotiator, you must learn to recognize them and set them aside. They have less than zero value to you as a serious negotiator.

Your Positive Expectations Are Killers

How many times have you heard one of these statements from your adversary:

"It looks good."
"That's exactly what we need."
"No question this is superior."
"Let's get together and wrap this up."
"Boy, you're just in time. Do we need you!"
"Do you think you can deliver five thousand by next month?"

"Well, this isn't set in concrete."
"You folks are right on target."
"This is in the groove—fits right in with where we're trying to go."

With all such remarks—and they are infinite in their variety; any businessperson with much experience could rattle dozens off the top of the head—your adversary is building your positive expectations to close the deal. If you buy into these statements, he'll move right in and take the advantage.

"It looks good." When the novice on the other side of the table hears such a statement, he starts mentally counting coup and then gets whipsawed by the next statement, "What's going to be your discounted price?" The novice provides some number and there he is, locked in for the rest of the negotiation unless he's really good, and he's not really good or he wouldn't have talked price at such an early stage of the negotiation, before he knew anything at all. Happens all the time.

In a recent negotiation I coached, the other team said they needed our best price on thirty-three thousand units. Everyone at the table knew that the going price for this expensive widget was somewhere around $1,000 per. The adversary told my client that although they had other suppliers for this item, they really wanted to give us the whole order so that they could get the best price. What happens when a negotiator is given the scent of such an order? If we're not careful, the first thing that pops into our mind is the number $33,000,000. Even with a volume discount thrown in, even for a large multinational, this counts as real money. As new business, it would be a triumph for any negotiator. If we're not careful, the blank slate has just been wiped away by this positive expectation. And that's *exactly* what the other team was trying to do in this case—build our expectations.

Now say we *are* suckered in by our excitement and immediately give them our best discounted price for the 33,000 units, expecting them to jump on this number, sign the contract this afternoon, and open the champagne tonight. And say they don't jump—and they won't, because the champagne can wait and they've played this game a million times. Instead, they come back and announce that they've decided to spread the purchase of these units among several vendors after all. Moreover, they've miscalculated their inventory. Turns out they only need 10,000 new units, not 33,000, and they want us to supply only 3,000 of these at the same incredibly good unit price we just agreed to for an order *ten times as large*. And by the way, they hint broadly, they're going to be very disappointed if we don't give them that price, if we say "no."

Now what do we do?! Now what are our emotions? Now what good did all those positive expectations do us? If there is *one* classic maneuver played by large multinationals and shrewd dealers in all fields to take advantage of anxious adversaries, this is the one. Build positive expectations with pie-in-the-sky numbers, then start in with the ifs, ands, and buts.

A specific case in point regarding expectations dates from a few years back, when I coached a small, $8 million company in its negotiation with a very large Irish firm. My team of four negotiators traveled to Ireland for a meeting—a $20,000 total expense probably, not inconsiderable for this small company. When they arrived, the Irish folks were suddenly unavailable. Pure gamesmanship? Perhaps. In any event, many negotiators would have let the prospect of this meeting drive up their positive expectations and, confronted with this disappointment, have started thinking in terms of, "Well, we're here, and we don't want to waste this trip." Then who knows what decisions they would have made. But my team had blank slated, they had *not* flown over with high expectations, and so had no qualms about saying, in effect, "Hey, it doesn't matter." They turned right around and flew home the following day. A few days later they calmly wrote a letter expressing their understanding that emergencies do happen, setting forth a new agenda, and inviting the Irish team to fly over here for the next meeting.

Which they did.

But positive expectations are so *positive*. They feel so good. Who doesn't want to be hopeful? I had one client who had an especially hard time ridding himself of positive expectations. For one thing, he had played tennis in high school and college and every coach he had along the way extolled the virtues of a positive attitude. "Positive attitude" sounds great, but to me it's just another, more seductive way of saying "positive expectations." For the negotiator, even a positive attitude is dangerous. Yes, it's true. It can devolve quickly into neediness, into positive expectations. When I teach blank slate, I mean *blank* slate. And it's hard.

Your Negative Expectations Are Also Killers

What about negative expectations? What about the string of double bogeys or double faults, or the series of lost deals? What happens to the emotional state of individuals stuck in these ruts? If they're not very careful they become rattled and emotional. Very likely, initial positive expectations now give way to negative expectations which can have a terribly debilitating effect. The dreaded S word—slump—comes to mind. Surely negative expectations play some role when we go into a slump—and negotiators, certainly those in direct sales, do have slumps.

In negotiations, your adversary may try to draw you into positive expectations, as we have seen, or they may try to draw you into negative expectations before things even get started. Consider this deal: A large contractor wants to buy a piece of equipment that usually sells for $1.7 million. Since they sometimes subcontract the work with a company that buys large numbers of these machines, they know that the discounted price for large orders is $1.3 million per unit. Now they want the same discounted price for their purchase of just one unit, and they stipulate this at the very beginning of negotiations. The untrained negotiator will hear this stipulation and immediately have a negative expectation of either no deal at all or a deal so heavily discounted that it might as well be no deal at all. The trained negotiator, meanwhile, has no thoughts either way about the final price for the machine. The trained negotiator recognizes those early numbers for what they are: early numbers of no real significance. The trained negotiator knows that there's nothing in his mission and purpose about busting the rate sheet just because this company wants him to, and he says, "Gee, we're sorry, we just can't sell the one machine to anyone, even you folks, with whom we'd love to do business, for $1.3 million. Maybe you could try to buy a used machine from your friends with the other company, or get them to order an extra machine in their next order, and then you could buy it from them. That might take some time, but wouldn't that work for you?"

This negotiator has blank slated and nurtured, and now waits for the reply.

Perhaps the most pervasive, straightforward example of negative expectations is when you're dealing with someone, or with an entire company, that has always been difficult to work with, badgered you to death, more trouble than they were worth. This is what you feel after every negotiation with these adversaries. Well, maybe they *are* more trouble than they're worth, and if they are you make that decision and cut your losses. But you do so calmly and rationally, not because these people are a pain in the ass. Tomorrow they may *not* be a pain in the ass, for whatever reason.

Remember from chapter 5 my client in San Francisco who paid a visit to the diabetic guy once a month for two years? He had every reason to develop negative expectations. If the visit hadn't been so convenient and easy, he probably would have said good-bye for good. But keeping in touch was no trouble, and he didn't succumb to negative expectations, and eventually he concluded that negotiation to everyone's satisfaction. However, my client's grade could be marked down for failing to find out exactly why this guy acted like he did in the morning. If he had blank slated, he could have saved some time off those two years of waiting.

Neither positive nor negative expectations have a place in my system. You blank slate and you *negotiate,* that's all. When you have a mission and purpose in place, when you have behavioral goals in place, when you've established your plan to solve the real problem, when you have laserlike focus—when you have all this going for you, why would you want to climb on any kind of emotional roller coaster of expectations? Once you really start using my system, you are so dedicated to goals over which you have control, so oblivious to anything over which you don't have control, and so free of neediness that expectations shouldn't even enter into the equation.

But of course they do anyway. Expectations are everywhere. In this regard, they're like emotions. In fact, they *are* emotions. You cannot banish them once and for all, but you can see them for what they are and take appropriate measures. When things seem to be going your way in a negotiation, it's easy to get excited and tempting to let your emotions take over. When you feel this happening, call a time-out, take a bathroom break, or suggest a break for coffee or for lunch, or step back in some other way.

Oh, come on, I've had students say. Blank slating can't be that big a deal. They sense the discipline required, and this scares them a little. It should. Discipline is difficult. But without discipline, you will never be a great negotiator. You will leave money on the table time after time.

Assume *Nothing*

Now what about assumptions, the other chief obstacle to effective blank slating? They're just as dangerous as positive and negative expectations, and just as common, because most of us come to believe that we're pretty good at reading other people, at understanding what they're really feeling and thinking. Negotiators, in particular, tend to pride themselves on their people skills. A thousand times I've heard someone say:

> *"I know what they'll do if we make that offer."*
> *"This is the way they operate."*
> *"If you raise the price, they'll want a volume discount."*
> *"I'm pretty sure she makes the decisions over there."*
> *"There's no way they'll make an offer today."*

There are just a million assumptions out there, lying in wait to ambush us. I learned my first lesson on the subject growing up in western Pennsylvania, where hunting was a way of life for a boy. When I got my first shotgun—a .410 bought by Cousin Earl

from the Sears catalog—I turned it over carefully in my hands. I
can still vividly picture the scene. Many readers probably have
the same memory. And I remember my father's first words to
me: "Check and see if it's loaded. Never assume a gun is not
loaded. Always check for yourself."

We're all vulnerable to assumptions, despite the fact that
we can all identify ones that have been flat-out wrong. In
Kosovo, NATO thought Slobodan Milošević would cave in after
a few high-altitude bombing sorties against isolated army barracks,
while Milošević thought that NATO politics would limit the
alliance to these same few high-altitude bombing sorties against
isolated army barracks. The results of these assumptions—
delusions might be the better word in this context—were tragic.
In the Vietnam War, our leaders assumed that if we stopped
bombing during the Christmas holidays, Ho Chi Minh would
draw back as well. This incorrect assumption cost about three
thousand lives in one week. Back at the turn of the century, vil-
lage blacksmiths who were married to the horse and buggy assumed that they were in a lot of trouble, but other blacksmiths
saw nothing but opportunity from the newfangled automo-
biles—opportunity in the form of service stations and repair
bills. They were able and willing to see things new, to see things
as they now were, to blank slate and thereby to seize opportunity. In 1982, air traffic controllers assumed that President
Reagan wouldn't have the guts to lock them out. Ouch. The
baseball umpires, as mentioned in chapter 4, assumed that the
often incompetent major-league bureaucracy wouldn't have
the guts to accept their resignations. Ouch. In chapter 3, I mentioned Bill Gates's brilliant decision to acknowledge that he and
Microsoft had been wrong to ignore the Internet. But what had
happened there in the first place? A failure to blank slate, plain

and simple. Coming from a software background, Bill Gates and his minions had failed to see that the Net could be bigger than the PC operating system, perhaps even make it obsolete eventually. Close call, Bill.

Maybe the favorite of all my stories among the folks who take one of my workshops concerns one Samuel Langley, who knew everything about the steam engine back at the turn of the twentieth century. He knew that steam was the ultimate power source for the foreseeable future. He just *knew* it. Therefore he tried to power an airplane with a steam engine. Langley was laughably wrong, in retrospect, but he went on to become a critical inventor in the world of aviation. How? By doing a lot of things we've talked about in previous chapters. He was able to hear the world say "no" to him in the form of failed experiments; he was able to embrace failure; he was able to set activity goals he could manage, not ends he could not control—such as powering an airplane with a steam engine; and he was able to blank slate and start all over. When the solution to powered flight proved to be the gasoline engine, not the steam engine, Langley embraced the new knowledge. If he had continued along the dead-end road that was his steam engine, he would never have contributed to aviation, and Langley Air Force Base in Virginia would now be named for someone else.

And now a final story that is also well received in my workshops, but without pleasure. In the 1960s, experts who knew everything about rockets and missiles were absolutely positive that aerial combat in the future would only be fought from a great distance. Close-in dogfighting was ancient history. Airplanes would fly at supersonic speeds, radar would see the enemy, missiles would be launched from many miles away, and battles would be won and lost by pilots who never saw the enemy planes. The engineers and experts were so certain this was correct that they built the first fighter aircraft in the history of aerial combat that was not equiped with a machine gun or rapid firing cannon. That was the F-4 Phantom. Guess what. Over North Vietnam, the lighter Soviet MiGs got in close where the American missiles weren't effective and sometimes shot down the bigger, less maneuverable, and *gunless* F-4. The horrible mistaken assumption surfaced quickly, and the vision of the solution was all too clear. But it took *nine months* to retro-arm the F-4s with a simple gun. The so-called experts just didn't know what they didn't know. They were incapable of blank slating. A tragic mistake for many of America's finest young men.

Back to business. How many times have you made the steam engine mistake and failed to correct your error? How many times have you gone into a meeting for one reason, only to find out that you were there for a completely different reason? How many times have you looked at the way someone was dressed and made an assumption, good or bad, that you later discovered was completely wrong? When was the last time you made an assumption based on the car someone was driving? We're talking Columbo here, of course: You never want to make the mistake that his suspects make, underestimating him. Anyone with much experience in business can recall when they didn't even bother calling on a potential client or supplier or customer because they assumed this deal would never work out, only to learn later that it might well have worked out. We've all done that—except, perhaps, Stanley Marcus, who preached to his sales force to treat every customer as if he or she were a million-aire, because he or she might indeed be a millionaire, certainly so in oil-rich Texas.

Actually, assumptions are perhaps even more dangerous than

expectations, because they're so subtle and insidious. If I say the word "retirement," what do I mean? If I say, "I'll pay you two dollars," what would you think? If I say, "I'm too busy to do this," what do you do? Every day such statements are made, and every day we make assumptions when we hear them. "Retirement"? The word can mean a million things. You don't know what *I* mean until you ask questions (interrogative-led questions such as "Why do you want to retire?"). If you accepted my $2 without question, you made an assumption that I wouldn't pay more than $2, and I never said I wouldn't. If you believed me when I said I was too busy, you assumed that I was telling the truth, and you assumed you knew what I meant by the word. But what does "busy" mean to me? Could we have different definitions? Of course we could. You have to find out.

Now let's play another workshop game. Close your eyes and picture a horse. Okay, what color is the horse? Is it light or dark? Shiny or dull? How big is the horse? How tall? How wide is he across the back? Oops! Did you recognize when I made my first assumption? Sure you did if you pictured a *mare* and I said "he." Because I pictured "he" when I posed the situation, I assumed you did as well. That's when I blew the blank slate. In a real negotiation that mistake could put me in a losing position. If you were in the horse business and were looking for a filly and I was picturing a gelding, we're not off to a good start. I needed to see *your* picture of the horse, not my picture. Forget my picture. It doesn't matter at all. But all too often we make this very mistake. Any one of us could sit down in the evening for ten minutes and make a list of the assumptions we made that day. Assumptions are like expectations in that we can't get rid of them, but as good negotiators we can beware of them.

We can also *plant* assumptions—and if the opposing parties let you, why not? Say you're asked how much your widget costs. "It's expensive," you say. Well, this word means very different things to a millionaire and to a man making $30,000, and—here's the important kicker—each immediately *assumes* that you mean what he means, and you may well find him preparing to pay a price much higher than yours. In fact, people—negotiators—make offers higher than you ever dreamed they would because of such false assumptions on their part.

> *"When can this be done?"*
> *"Soon."*

Well, "soon" can mean anything. When you're told "soon," you have to find out. Ask a question. When you say "soon," you can take advantage of the fact that your adversaries don't find out. Our assumptions always work against us. Their assumptions can work for us.

Do Your Research

Research can rid us of many assumptions and help us blank slate, but we don't have the habit of doing research. Instead, we allow ourselves to be led by assumptions. The lack of information makes it easy to assume and almost impossible to blank slate. Not knowing about something, you have the urge to fill in the blanks with the first thing that pops into your mind. You wing it, so to speak.

But not the Japanese. Before they go into any negotiation they do in-depth research, sending out teams to study and gather facts about the companies and the markets involved. But we Americans often skip this vital step. I am constantly amazed at how many negotiations are conducted without even the most basic research: going to the Web, to the business papers and magazines, to the financial statements and year-end reports in order to study the adversary and find out its financial position, its strengths and weaknesses in the marketplace, its major profit (or loss) centers. A client in Silicon Valley mentioned the other day that he is constantly amazed at how his negotiating team outprepares teams from Fortune 100 companies—Fortune *100,* not 500—the biggest and therefore, presumably, among the best companies we have to offer.

On the other hand, the supply systems management teams from aggressive multinationals *will* have done copious research. You can pretty much assume that they know every competitor for your product or service and the financial condition of those competitors, their strengths and weaknesses, their negotiating strategy, their negotiating success, the decision-making hierarchy, and personal details about the key decision makers—education, college, awards, family, pets, golf handicap, and so on.

It follows that you must have the same information about your adversary and your competitors, doesn't it? There is just no excuse in failing to learn all you can about everything relating to your field of business in general and this negotiation in particular, but if you enter a negotiation with a win-win frame of mind, are you going to feel the necessity all that strongly? I doubt it.

We now have even less excuse for failing to do research than we used to. Twenty years ago, the library was a few blocks away. What a chore! Today, the Web is right in front of us, on our desks. Use it. That said, the low-tech newspaper remains an invaluable resource. Did you know that the North Vietnamese used a network of Americans to gather "harmless" news releases on local young men during the Vietnam War? They stockpiled this information in case some of these men became their prisoners of war. And some of them did. And some of them were broken with the help of this information about family and home. A horrible example of the power of applied research.

A much more pleasant example is provided by Coach Woody Hayes of Ohio State, whom I had the privilege of knowing in the 1960s and 1970s. Coach Hayes was one of the greatest football coaches who ever lived, but that's secondary. He was also one of the greatest individuals of his era. He had an enormous impact on my life, as he had on the lives of thousands of others. He had an enormous impact on my ideas for negotiation. Coach Hayes was an indefatigable reader of newspapers. Today he would be a master of the Web universe, without a doubt. He used his research to impress, persuade, educate, and demonstrate that being a great coach required more than just winning football games. At the hundred-year commemoration of the death of Ralph Waldo Emerson, Harvard University chose Coach Hayes—yes, Woody Hayes, college football coach—to be the keynote speaker, at which time he used his vast stores of research to compare the lessons of Emerson to our modern-day problems. He received a standing ovation.

Now let's recall that negotiation from earlier in this chapter, the one in which the adversary wants the same volume discount for three thousand widgets that our company usually gives for much larger orders. Mentioning the number thirty-three thousand early in the negotiation was intended to drive up my client's positive expectations, and against many negotiators this time-tested trick might have worked. But my team had done its research. It knew that the multinational's total worldwide capacity for these widgets was only *twenty-two thousand* units. The nerve! Those negotiators never intended to procure thirty-three

thousand widgets. They were only interested in driving up expectations and thereby extracting a price they could then use for
leverage. Thanks to research, thanks to blank slating, this gambit
didn't work with my clients. They knew there wasn't going to be
an order for thirty-three thousand units, so they hadn't gotten
excited. They said instead, "No, sorry, we can't help you with
those three thousand widgets at such a steep discount."

It Couldn't Be Simpler

Research is indispensable, but the best single, easy-to-use, fool-
proof tool we have at our disposal to blank slate is the simplest
one imaginable: taking great notes. By its very nature, if we stop
to think about the process, note taking removes us from our
world and keeps us in our adversary's world. The simple act of
picking up the pen or pencil moves us in that direction. Note
taking reinforces listening skills. As we take our notes, our con-
centration is automatically focused on what is being said. In
seminars, meetings, and negotiations, I can quickly tell which
ones are the most successful people around the table. They are
effectively silencing their own thoughts and learning as much as
they can about their adversary's world. They are the ones listening closely and taking notes. They are blank slating and gather-
ing the pieces of the puzzle. (It's important to note that they are
not *solving* the puzzle. That comes later, with analysis, with
burning the midnight oil.) They know that what is *really said* and
what we *actually hear* during a negotiation is far more important
than what we allow ourselves to think while others talk. In order
to blank slate effectively, the little voice in our own heads must
be silent.

If we take notes, we have to be listening. We all think we're good listeners, but when was the last time you focused on your listening skills just for practice? You must listen to every word just as closely as a trial lawyer listens to every word of testimony without letting the mind wander off, without thinking about what you want to say next, without interrupting, without answering your own questions. I'm not much of a Freudian, but Freud did preach to his pupils that they must adopt the same approach with their patients: First just *listen* with the most open possible mind. Don't judge. That comes later.

As we take our notes, our emotions are more easily controlled. Our nerves relax, our stomach quiets down, we comfortably settle into the negotiating session. We don't show excitement or disappointment. As we take notes, we are also allowing the adversary to be more okay, by making her feel more important because we are taking notes on what *she* has to say. And then, on the plain practical side, notes are our documentation of what was said—and also what was done or gestured, because great note takers make note of nonverbal behavior and moods.

How many times have you found yourself unable to remember a point? You might have gotten the gist of it but can't remember specifics. You're left with some holes in the conversation, perhaps even a general vagueness. Worse yet, when was the last time you found yourself wondering who you just talked to, because you hadn't written down someone's name? Was it Sue or Sally? Jim or John?

Most people can scribble down a few notes here and there in a conversation, but taking great notes takes lots of practice. The next meeting you go to, pull out your legal pad instead of your business card. Next time the phone rings, pick up your pen, really listen, and take notes—even if it's your mother on the line.

(That might be the ultimate challenge—trying to blank slate with a close member of your family!)

If we take notes, we're listening, which is good, and we're not talking, which is equally good. No talking! This is one of my cardinal rules—and an exaggeration, as I admitted earlier. I don't mean that you can't utter a word, but I do mean that in a negotiation most of us should talk a lot less than we do, in the interest of controlling neediness, in the interest of blank slating. When we are spare with our words, we are able to ask much more focused questions, which keep us on track and give us clearer pictures. If you can't keep from talking, you won't be able to blank slate.

Not talking is hard. We're trained through education to know all the answers and to blurt them out at the first opportunity. We have been rewarded time and time again for knowing the correct answer. Our life has revolved around our intelligence. We go to great pains to let people know what we know. But the danger here is easily illustrated. We've all been to social functions where someone seems to know it all, and he makes the ridiculous assumption that people enjoy hearing him unload his vast stores of knowledge. But what really happens when you find yourself trapped in that situation with that guy? For one thing, you may feel unokay and get a little defensive and resentful and turn him off entirely. How seriously do you take him? How much do you remember of what he said? Talk about a bad assumption: His assumption that you'll be impressed by all his talking literally takes him out of the game. (Here's another assumption, on my part this time: This blowhard/gasbag/know-it-all will be a man. Funny about that.)

Spilling the Beans

So, no talking, or *less* talking. As a negotiator, if you can't control the motor mouth you're eventually going to say something
you'll regret for the duration of that negotiation. Communica-
tion by e-mail is often preferred to a phone call, especially for a
beginning negotiator, because it reduces emotion. It also reduces
the possibility of spilling your beans in the lobby. That's the
phrase I use for the mistaken revelation of information: "spilling
the beans." When it happens the next time, just make sure it's
from the other side, not from you. If you conduct many negotiations you *will* be the happy recipient of spilled beans. That's because many people *knowingly* spill beans as they fight for the
feeling of self-importance. Kind of pitiful, but true. People also
spill beans in the very mistaken belief that this will help advance
their own position or agenda, like in *The Godfather, Part II,* when
poor, weak Fredo spills to Hymen Roth (by way of Johnny Olla)
details about Michael Corleone's position in the negotiation, all
because Olla assured Fredo there'd be something in it for him if
the negotiations were successfully concluded. Beans get spilled
all over the place, that's the truth, and your job is to gather up all
those beans and put them to good use.

As it happens, I have something of a pet peeve regarding
spilled beans in a very specific situation: putting forth a full financial package for a highest-level corporate officer before getting a commitment from the candidate to accept or reject that
package. Often, officers looking for a new colleague feel they
have to offer the package before asking for the commitment.
They feel the package drives the negotiation. But what happens
is that the candidate takes the spilled beans—the financial package offer—back to his current employer and uses it for leverage.

Happens all the time. I urge a different approach. I urge my clients to say to the candidate, "We're going to commit to a financial package that will be at the top of the industry, but we're not going to reveal it until we have your commitment to take it or reject it. We don't want this package to be used to start a bidding war with your current company." This is a fair approach, but companies are afraid they'll lose the candidate, so they spill the beans, and then they lose the candidate *because* they spilled the beans when he uses the package for leverage and re-ups with his current company.

Often people blatantly tell you they are about to spill vital beans.

"I shouldn't really say this, since I work for Intrepid, but I agree with your company's reaction. Our side has made some really dramatic statements, but this is all about negotiation. We pay penalties when we are late and we expect our suppliers to share part of that if they are late for us. We don't really plan to sue you into the ground if you are late, but we have to start the agreement somewhere."

"Richard would not want to hear me talking to you, but we are looking for you to have some cash in the game—does not have to be ten percent—we pulled that number out of the air. What's the first rule in negotiating? Always ask for more than what you are willing to take. So we did. But it does not have to be ten percent. I don't know what is has to be. Could be software, spares, service, a credit toward other products, I don't know. We just want to make sure you are committed to executing."

"Tom would probably kill me for saying this . . . but the truth is that he loves your product. The technology will solve all of our needs today. Period. That is a fact."

In the dance company negotiation I've followed off and on since chapter 3, one of the program director's thirty-minute monologues with the booking agent divulged that one of the agent's colleagues had advised the director that her organization was not the only one that had not signed a contract. What a situation: The director was spilling beans about spilled beans. (And the information about the original beans was wrong, to boot.)

I have to admit that I'd be very surprised—flabbergasted—if any client of mine committed the same error. It's just so foolish. But Lord knows they have ample opportunity. I have mentioned the cozy relationships that many corporate negotiators try to establish with their adversaries, for the sake of establishing a subtle neediness on the adversary's part. Another purpose of these "close" relationships is the opportunity they pose for collecting spilled beans.

"Say, Joe, is that pricing structure you guys just proposed for real?"

Or maybe it's some remark that's just a little leading—"Boy, Joe, that's a bear of a position you guys took last week"—in the hope that you, by way of friendship, might slip and reply, "Well, you know how the game is played, Pete."

We've seen how negotiators use hints of huge purchases, future global alliances, and the like to set up naive win-win negotiators with neediness and false expectations, but another point of these promises is to get you to spill your beans about internal cost-profit structures. This is basic cost optimization strategy: Hey, we're partners. Let us help you hold your costs down.

It's tough to let go of expectations, not to assume, to listen instead of talking, to take copious notes all the time, to be certain not to spill beans. But with training and practice, blank slate can become a behavioral goal and discipline for anyone. There's definitely no excuse for the careful negotiator's spilling the beans. With dedication and practice, you can make sure that your slate is erasable and easily adjusted. You will develop the habit of constantly reviewing the status of the negotiation. When your picture changes, you'll change with it. But even if you're good at blank slating, have no expectations and no assumptions, listen well, take great notes, refrain from excessive talking, and don't spill beans—even if you're the perfect blank slater, the world outside the negotiation can *still* intrude on your ability to blank slate. If you're overly tired, it's difficult to focus. If you're dealing with the remains of the night before, blank slating is difficult. If there's a crisis in your home, blank slating can be impossible. If you feel you cannot blank slate for any reason, you have only one option: cancel the negotiating session. This is how important the blank slate is.

Play a Mind Game

When you were a small child, did you ever see a pony in the clouds, or perhaps the face of a clown? When you read *Robin Hood,* did you literally see Friar Tuck fall in the river? Did you see yourself shoot the arrow that won the archery contest? It's this ability to envision that we had as children that we must now cultivate as negotiators. When we blank slate we can truly see, as if for the first time. Through my work with hundreds of students and in hundreds of actual negotiations over the last many years, I have learned that the ability to envision varies with individuals. I also know that the ability to envision is directly linked to the level of success we can achieve. The greater the ability to envision, the greater the potential for success. If you can't see it, you'll never be able to do it.

Everyone can see better than they do now. There are many simple exercises that help us do so. Consider the word *sky*. Say it to yourself, close your eyes, see the sky you want to see. All of us have a favorite sky. Pick another word for a phenomenon in the natural world. See that phenomenon. Turn it around in your mind's eye. When you get the chance—but sometime soon—go to the movies without leaving your favorite chair: Find a quiet place and relax, close your eyes, and run a movie in your mind of some pleasant time in your life (a sporting event, a date, a fun time in school or at work). Before a negotiation, see that negotiation unfolding in your mind. Picture yourself asking the questions, taking the notes, and negotiating with perfect behavior. See yourself relaxed with no expectations, no need, and no fear—a perfectly blank slate. It works, even for a hard-nosed corporate negotiator.

9

Know Their "Pain," Paint Their "Pain"

Work with Your Adversary's Real *Problem*

YOUR ADVERSARY IN any negotiation must have vision before they can ever take action. I've said it before, I'll say it again: no vision, no action. No vision, no decision. No vision, no deals that stick. This is Human Nature 101, and it's the subtext, to one extent or another, of much of the preceding material. But what, exactly, do we need a vision *of*?

Pain. This is what brings every adversary in every negotiation to the table. I realize it's a harsh word, maybe even offensive to some who perhaps feel it makes negotiation and business into a blood sport. I appreciate this concern, but all too often negotiations *do* become extremely emotional and can require extremely tough decisions. I use pain only as a *technical* term. It has nothing to do with actual physical pain (although it could certainly lead to that, in the form of headaches and upset stomachs). In my system, pain is whatever the negotiator sees as *the current or future problem*. People make decisions in order to alleviate and take away this current or future problem—this pain. Put in these terms, what else would any negotiation concern?

I want to start digging into this subject with a brief history lesson. In my work with clients, I've found that these lessons are a great way to make a couple of points. First, many critical moments in history are really negotiations, if we consider carefully, and we can learn lessons from them that apply to our more mundane endeavors. Second, setting a new principle in a context of great historical importance helps to emphasize the importance of the principle. It gets people's attention.

One story from history that gets people's attention is the story of Winston Churchill's brilliant success in getting the attention of the worldwide public in the first days of World War II. On May 13, 1940, after Churchill had become British prime minister following the resignation of Neville Chamberlain, whose name has since become synonymous with appeasement, the new leader of the British polity appeared before the House of Commons and was asked for a succinct statement of his wartime policy. His answer: "It is to wage war, by sea, land, and air, with all our might and with all the strength that God can give us: to wage war against a monstrous tyranny, never surpassed in the dark, lamentable catalogue of human crime. That is our policy."

To whom was Churchill directing that remark? With whom was he negotiating? Not with Hitler. To hell with Hitler, literally. No, the new prime minister was negotiating with the constituencies of his potential allies in the democratic West. The free world had been and still was, at that time, little prepared for the massive German industrial and military might that steam-rolled Europe. Chamberlain was convinced there was no hope against Hitler's war machine, and he had therefore compromised the British Empire in his efforts to avoid a war he did not think he could win. So it was no surprise that Churchill inherited a constituency that saw no hope. He did have hope, however, and passion, and genius, and his problem was how to persuade his people and their ostensible allies on the other side (our side) of the Atlantic. His solution was expressed on June 14, 1940, when he spoke again on the subject of the day:

> *Even though large tracts of Europe and many old and famous States have fallen or may fall into the grip of the Gestapo and all the odious apparatus of Nazi rule, we shall not flag or fail. We shall go on to the end, we shall fight in France, we shall fight on the seas and oceans, we shall fight on with growing confidence and growing strength in the air, we shall defend our island, whatever the cost may be, we shall fight on the beaches, we shall fight on the landing grounds, we shall fight in the fields and in the streets, we shall fight in the hills; we shall never surrender, and even if, which I do not for a moment believe, this island or a large part of it were subjugated and starving, then our Empire beyond the seas, armed and guarded by the British Fleet, would carry on the struggle, until, in God's good time, the new world, with all its power and might, steps forth to the rescue and the liberation of the old.*

I don't know about you, but I get chills thinking about the passion behind Churchill's righteous campaign against Hitler. His words in this speech are the perfect way to introduce the subject of pain in a negotiation. With a towering passion and 179 perfectly chosen words, Churchill wanted to paint a picture for his vast audience of the *pain* of living under—bowing down before—abominable tyranny. He also wanted to paint a second picture, that of fighting against this abomination with, if necessary, the life of the last good man and woman on earth. His adversary was the constituency of the Western democracies, and they were never going to make the decision to go to war without a clear *vision* of the intolerable *pain* that would follow from Nazi rule.

Just recently a friend told me about a speech he had heard by Hugh L. McColl Jr., chairman and CEO of Bank of America, before the Economic Club in Chicago. McColl had been in banking forty-one years, starting with a small one in North Carolina, building what is now Bank of America. A member of the audience asked how McColl had successfully negotiated over one hundred mergers and acquisitions, and he answered, "I really try to get inside their head before I ever get in the room with them." Exactly! And what was McColl looking for inside the adversary's head? The pain, to use my nomenclature.

As a negotiator you can and will make a lot of mistakes, of course, but your clear vision of your adversary's pain will see you through thick and thin. As I stated earlier, adhering to your mission and purpose will keep you from going seriously astray in a *negative* direction. Now you have a tool for keeping you oriented in a *positive* direction: your vision of your adversary's pain. With both mission and purpose and pain you're in great shape, but without both you're wandering in the desert.

One day quite a few years ago my son Jim and I were tooling along on an errand for my wife, Patty, in Dublin, Ohio, where we lived (and a suburb of Columbus), when we passed the local exotic car dealership just as one of those transport trucks was unloading some new Porsches. One of these beauties was flaming red, with a black convertible top. Light rain had moistened the top and beaded on the body. Now the sun was out, and that car was glistening. "Jimbo," I exclaimed, "look at that. Porsche doesn't make a convertible. They only build T-tops and coupés. Where did this convertible come from? I'll bet someone had it built by special order. There couldn't be another one like it in Ohio, much less here in Dublin."

I ended up buying that car. Why? The picture I had of myself as the only guy in Ohio with this magnificent Porsche, cruising down the road in that machine on a sunny day with the top down and with heads turned wherever I went. My pain was my ego trip, my vanity. I ached for this car. Okay, no harm in falling into the position of needing a car. Silly, maybe, but not all that harmful. But in a negotiation, pain is big-time serious. This is why I use that harsh word, to emphasize the seriousness of the concept. In every negotiation, "pain" is what brings the negotiator to the table in the first place. It is, in effect, the soft underbelly in his negotiating position, the most vulnerable point.

Your pain in a negotiation can be your need to put this particular machine on your factory floor and not one of the competitive products. But maybe you don't know that you need *this particular machine;* maybe all you understand is that you need a pretty good machine. My primary job in this negotiation is to create vision of your *real* pain, that this is the only machine for your purposes, that this technology is the future of this industry, and that without it your efficiency and your business plan will suffer. Meanwhile, my own pain in this negotiation is that my company has committed 60 percent of its resources to the development of this machine, and we want to establish it as the new industry standard. Our adversaries, if they're on top of things, will make sure that we know that they know that we've bet the farm on this machine. They will have found this out through research, of course.

Other scenarios: Your pain can be your desire to hire this particular person, who is head and shoulders above any other candidate you've interviewed; or, on the other side, it can be your desire as the applicant to get this particular job because the salary is twice what you're making now. Or the pain can be your desire as an editor to buy a particular manuscript from an author because it's the best "airport novel" you've read in years, or it can be your burning desire to sell this airport novel for major money, because you've gone through your life's meager savings while writing it for the past two years. It can be your desire to sell this Porsche *today,* not tomorrow, or it can be your desire to be the only big shot in Ohio driving this model. It can be a dance company's need to book this gig because they need the revenue and it fills out the schedule, or it can be the need of the performing arts theater to fill in the blank on their own schedule. It can be the football player's burning desire to play for a top program, or it can be the desire of the coach of the top program to get this particular kid for his team. And in his negotiation with his people, Winston Churchill had his own pain as well: his picture of what failure meant, not to him personally, but to Western Europe and beyond.

(In the political and moral realm, you could almost define leadership as the effective painting of the pain *shared* by leader and people. Think of Lincoln: He had to share with his constituents his own picture of the pain that would follow if the Union were allowed to disintegrate. Of course, Winston Churchill and Abraham Lincoln were two of the greatest men who ever lived. Each understood in his *hara,* his gut, that all meaningful actions and decisions begin with a *vision.* Without the vision each painted with his incomparable words, there would have been no decisive action by the people. We more limited individuals could do worse than learn from Lincoln and Churchill.)

In a really efficient negotiation, *both* parties will work to clarify the vision of the pain of the adversary. In any event, you must never enter a negotiation in which you haven't seen your adversary's pain. *Never.* In fact, if your mission and purpose is set in the world of the adversary—and it is, of course—then the features and benefits of what you offer in this negotiation will necessarily be addressed to the pain in the adversary's world. That said, you must never forget to blank slate and make certain that there's no hidden pain that you haven't discovered and that is subverting the entire deal.

In many cases, the pain will be pretty straightforward and the issues pretty clear. But sometimes you really have to dig. The purchase of life insurance comes to mind. I can think of a simple reason someone might give the salesman setting up an appointment—"Well, I guess my wife and kids just need some life insurance"—but I can see that hidden behind this general emotion could be a host of particular circumstances, and it would be the particular circumstance, not the general emotion, that generates the deal in the end.

You May Have to Really Hunt for the Pain

In most cases in which you have an intractable problem in a negotiation, either you have failed to help your adversary understand his pain, or you have failed to have a clear vision of the pain, or the real pain is actively hidden.

In big corporate negotiations, imagine the different people and their private agendas in which the real pain would be carefully camouflaged. Divisions within a large corporation will even hide their pain from other divisions *within the same corporation*— common bureaucratic behavior—much less from negotiators for other companies. Negotiators definitely don't hang the pain out for just anyone to look at. Well, occasionally they do, but probably they don't, and great professional negotiators never will. People—negotiators—have to feel safe in order to reveal their pain and, perhaps, even to see it clearly themselves. They definitely will not expose their pain if they think the adversary will try to take advantage of them. Who would? So your challenge as a negotiator is to discover and paint for your adversary the clearest possible picture of their pain *while always nurturing.*

According to family tradition, my great-grandfather used to say about one of the mules on his farm, "To get his attention you have to hit him between the eyes with a two-by-four. When you have his attention, he can see what he ought to do." But this doesn't work with us humans. We can be just as lacking in vision as mules, but we will not usually respond to the two-by-four. You want your human adversaries to see the pain, but you do not want to hit them between the eyes with it. You soften the blow, so to speak, with nurturing.

A classic example of how a clear vision of a hidden pain, revealed by nurturing, drives the decision-making process involved a client who was trying to acquire a much smaller company whose founder had recently died. However, the asking price per share for the company in play was three times the true market value of the stock. The price was so inflated that it made no sense. My client simply couldn't understand why the adversary would take such a risk with such a high asking price. Obviously, my client didn't have a clue when it came to the adversary's *real* pain.

As it turned out, the widow of the founder of that company belonged to the same club as one of my client's board members, whose wife often played cards with the widow. One day at the club, the board member's wife chatted up the widow and asked her how she was able to face dealing with all the details involving her late husband's company. The board member's wife asked this *interrogative*-led question *(How . . . ?)* in such a nurturing way that the widow spilled her beans. She revealed that the sale of her late husband's company represented, in her mind, the end of her husband's legacy, and she felt he would be forgotten. Her husband had been an inventor, and she was desperately trying to find a way to immortalize him, especially for her many grandchildren and great-grandchildren.

The board member's wife was able to set up a meeting between the widow and my client. The mission and purpose of that meeting for my client? To get the woman to see and describe what was *most* important to her and her family in this acquisition. My client explained to her that the two companies were so far apart in price that the difference could never be overcome. He asked her what he could do. *"How* can I help you?" he asked. For a second time, the widow spilled the beans and told my client about her fear of her husband's legacy disappearing. My client asked her if she had ever thought of erecting a memorial on the grounds of his company to recognize and honor his achievements. She was absolutely flabbergasted. My client added that if he made this acquisition, his company would be pleased to establish and pay for the memorial. She could choose the artist and the material and design this memorial in any way that she wanted. She accepted this offer almost on the spot, and within six months the acquisition was completed. My client had finally learned the real pain at the heart of the negotiation, and then had helped the woman see this pain in her own mind and proposed a way for her to alleviate it.

Turn on the discovery channel, I like to say. Paint the pain. When you finally get to the right person in a negotiation, they will often spill the beans and reveal their real pain so that you can fix it. That target company had valued itself at something approaching $100 million. Ridiculous, as we knew, but my client's board of directors eventually authorized $50 million for the purchase. In the end they paid less than $25 million.

And Don't Forget to Nurture

I have a number of clients in the digital world, where change comes so fast a company can find itself behind the eight ball almost overnight. (If it can happen to Microsoft, it can happen to anyone.) If you're convinced that a potential customer has taken a potentially fatal fork in the road, and you know that you have the means to help them correct that mistake, how in the world do you go about painting this terrible pain? How do you tell a company that has invested tens of millions of dollars that they've got to turn their supertanker on a dime, and quickly. You certainly can't say, "Folks, you've just wasted $30 million and several years' work by twenty good people. That's the bad news. The good news is that our technology can bail you out." That won't get you anywhere. You can't challenge all the time and money that the company has invested in a misguided direction without nurturing. Without careful nurturing, the vision your adversaries will have is that they're incompetent losers and that their heads will soon be rolling. Only with the most careful nurturing and with the most careful painting of the pain will they see and *accept* the merits of the correct vision, and see and *decide* that going in another direction is the only way for long-term success. So you say:

> *"Now, I ask you to be patient with me here, but I've got a real problem. Maybe I'm out of my mind. I need you to tell me if I am. Just say so. And everything I say is going to sound self-serving, I understand that, but with your permission, I'd like to tell you* what I see, *and together let's see if it makes sense."*

But you don't describe your vision at all. Instead, you ask a series of interrogative-led questions to build their vision. The first question is "What direction is this whole industry now going in the area of wireless widgets?" You have nurtured, you have given the adversary permission to say no, and you will use the 3+ technique. This is how you start building for your adversary his vision of his own pain, which in this case he isn't hiding and doesn't even know. By the way, the "he" here is not some hypothetical adversary. This was an actual meeting between the president of one of my clients and the president of a major corporation heading for serious trouble.

When you begin any new negotiation or find yourself losing control of an ongoing negotiation, you return to—what? Your mission and purpose. And where is your mission and purpose set? In your adversary's world. And what is embedded deep within your adversary's world? Their pain. When in doubt, return to the pain. And always nurture, because without it, the pain may simply be too much.

> *"Gee, that's a bad break. How long will your car be in the shop?"*
> *"That's terrible. How long will your company pay for the temporary apartment?"*
> *"This is great technology. You must really have invested a lot in it."*

"Sure we have a lot of competitors, so you're in good shape in that regard. Now when do you need to get your line back up and running?"

The *clearer* your adversary's vision of his pain, the *easier* the decision-making process. This may sound like one of the more counterintuitive aspects of my system of negotiation, but think about it this way: If your doctor doesn't paint for you a crystal-clear picture of your case—your pain—will she ever be able to "sell" you this medicine or this outpatient procedure, much less this three-hour operation? Somehow I rather doubt it.

I think about this psychological issue every time I see another advertisement in the antismoking campaign. How long have we been funding these programs now? How effective they have been, especially the ones aimed at kids? Even granting that they've helped a little, and I think this would be hard to prove, clearly they're not really effective. Why not? They have not been able to successfully paint a vision of the pains of smoking—the hacking cough, the odors, the cost, the public disapproval (in some circles), and the possibility of cancer—clearly enough to offset the pleasures and, of course, the *addiction.*

Painting Pain is Not *Creating* Pain

I hope it's understood that I'm not talking about *creating* pain in your adversary. Many times I've heard someone say, "Boy, did I put them in pain." That's ridiculous. You help create the vision, but you don't create the pain itself at all. The pain is just there. The doctor doesn't create your pain; she helps you see your case clearly.

The retail salesperson isn't starting from scratch. My son Jim and I didn't wander onto the parking lot of the Porsche dealership by accident. I wanted that Cabriolet badly. No salesman in the world was going to be able to convince me that I had an aching need I didn't really have. Likewise, no one wanders into an electronics store intent on buying a new refrigerator. The salesperson always has something to work with. And it wasn't as if Churchill had nothing to work with in his negotiation with his constituents. Western Europe and the United States did need to gear up for the war with Hitler. The British certainly knew the dangers posed by Hitler. They just needed their vision *and the solution* painted with passion. (Americans were a little slower on the uptake, but that was natural. We were far away and justifiably sick of European wars, but we, too, could finally be stirred to action by the combined efforts of Churchill and Roosevelt to paint with passion both the vision and the solution.)

So, please, forget any idea you may have about *creating* pain for your adversary. That's amateur hour. What you help to create is their *vision* of their very real pain. The difference is huge, and you shouldn't read further until you're convinced I'm right about this. As a negotiator, you want the adversary to see and understand his pain calmly and rationally, just as you have long ago seen and understood your own pain, calmly and rationally. (For example, am I wrong in presuming that you're reading this book because you have some kind of modest pain in the area of negotiation?) If you seem to be mired in an intractable problem in a negotiation, it's not because you haven't been able to *create* some pain. As I said earlier, you either don't have a clear vision of your adversary's pain, or you haven't been able to paint the picture clearly for your adversary—or the adversary doesn't even see their own pain!

"Oh, come on," you may blurt. But it's true. Sometimes the

adversary just doesn't get it. "But wouldn't this be good?" new clients have asked. "If I figure out their pain and they don't, doesn't this put me one up? Doesn't it allow me to sneak up on them?" No, this is poppycock. It's not real world. If the company on the other side of the table doesn't understand that they need your machine and no other machine, what's their incentive in the negotiation? If the real estate agent doesn't understand that this lunar-powered house in the middle of the lake is so quirky very few people will be interested, where's the incentive to come down from the ridiculous asking price? You think anyone is going to make a deal without a very clear vision of *why* they need to make this deal? Please. Their ignorance of their pain only puts everybody one *down*. If they don't know their own pain, they'll never make the deal.

Two competitors were trying to sell an apparently comparable piece of equipment to a third company. One's price was $2.9 million, the other's was $2.1 million. There was only one difference in the machines, which no one knew about at the beginning of the negotiations: The more expensive machine could be configured so that it would provide much longer service than the inexpensive machine. This longer service life was much more valuable than the $800,000 difference in the cost, but— unbelievably, perhaps—the buyer had failed to understand this basic point. When we were able to get the purchaser to see clearly their future pain if they purchased the less-expensive machine, to see that this had become a situation of pay me now or pay me later, they eagerly purchased the more expensive machine.

Another, more detailed story that vividly demonstrates the power of painting the *real* pain is the second installment of the Network, Inc., saga. You may recall from the first installment, related in chapter 2, that the company had gotten itself into a serious bind thanks to terrible negotiating that had produced contracts under which it was losing $100,000 on every machine shipped to its primary customer. But they had kept shipping for fear of losing this account and going out of business. Of course, losing money on every machine would also put them out of business, just more slowly. This situation played out during a downturn in the industry some years ago. Up against the wall at last, the Network board was prepared to shut down if one more machine was shipped at this losing price. The president was instructed to renegotiate or cancel the deal with a major European conglomerate.

The negotiators on the other side were real tigers. Their entire strategy for every negotiation was to play the win–win game, bludgeon their win–win adversaries, and drive down every price from their many suppliers. And they were successful in doing so. They had certainly succeeded against Network. Several members of the Network team were completely cowed by these negotiators, who, they were convinced, would get angry and walk away if Network tried to change its losing situation into a profitable one by renegotiating. In fact, these folks lost their jobs because they refused to go along with the new negotiating system I was coaching. But the president was ready to try anything.

We were short of time, so I worked intensely with the president, and he controlled his team accordingly. They had been introduced to my methods, but that was about all. They weren't really trained, but we forged ahead, because we had no choice. Seven days before Network was supposed to ship the first machine in a large order signed eight months earlier, we set up a conference call among thirteen negotiators in six countries. My client, Network's president, opened with minimal pleasantries because this was an ultraserious phone call. Nothing could be allowed to distract from that. His statement was short, concise, and direct:

"Our problem is that we want to be your supplier of the future. We want to be the provider of technology that takes you into the twenty-first century, but we must alert you that we cannot ship the machines currently under order to you, because we are losing $100,000 per machine. We are in a desperate situation. We simply cannot ship the machines."

The president closed his remarks by apologizing for putting the other company in this position, which as a professional businessman he would never do if it weren't a matter of his company's survival. If Network didn't survive, there wouldn't be any machines to ship at any price.

It's important to see that he did not explicitly paint the adversary's pain, but he didn't have to. By describing the desperate situation, by saying "No, we cannot deliver these machines at this price," he made it easy for the adversary to discover and feel his own current and future pain should *he* say "no" in return. Often there is no more effective way to paint the adversary's pain than by asking them to tell you "no." When your adversary carefully considers exactly what this "no" entails, their pain becomes very clear indeed, and good things can happen for you.

In this negotiation, the adversary had its very low price for the machines, but now there were consequences. First, they wouldn't get the equipment—and they did need these machines, which were state of the art, the very best. Second, they were in danger of driving this technically superior supplier out of business. Third, if they succeeded in doing this, they would lose their effective "dual vendor strategy" in negotiations. Given that there were only two suppliers of this vital equipment, the loss of one would mean they'd have no leverage with the remaining supplier. They'd put themselves at the mercy of the other supplier, in fact, whose machine was technically inferior to boot. *Then* where would their vaunted cost optimization strategies leave them? I'm sure the adversary's negotiators understood all this in a flash after the statement from the Network president.

You Cannot *Tell* Anyone Anything

Rather than set out on the sometimes long, hard road of painting vision and pain, many negotiators make the fatal mistake of thinking they can *convince* someone to make the rational decision to do something, to buy something, to see something the same way they see it. They offer up reasons, facts, figures, and charm that they are sure would make any rational person see things the way they see them. In fact, most negotiators think of the gift of gab as one of their greatest assets. But what's the problem with trying to convince someone to see the same thing you see? You know the answer to this question, but let's go ahead and spell it out. To begin with, you're asking your adversary to come into *your* world and to see *your* world. And where do we want to spend our time in a negotiation? In the adversary's world. Second, if we're busy giving reasons to our adversary, we're too busy talking; we're totally in our world and impeding our ability to blank slate. Finally, and most important of all, we're forgetting that decisions are made not with our head but with our heart and guts, first of all. Remember, negotiations are 100 percent emotional until a decision is made.

You cannot tell anyone anything. Think about this and be sure you agree with me. You can only help people *see for themselves.* To test this thesis, a clever client once devised a clever experiment. He was making a presentation to a financial analyst, and he did it twice, in effect—once in the standard didactic way, and then a second time in which he asked questions of the analyst. In the first presentation, the analyst sat quietly and took a few notes, but the second time around he filled page after page with notes as he engaged with the interrogatives from my client. Since that day, that particular client has understood completely the power of asking questions as a way of painting the vision, the pain, so the adversary in a negotiation sees it for his own.

In trying to convince someone to buy this product or service or to sign this deal, in trying to *reason* with someone, we are setting ourselves up to fail. Instead, we have to use our fuels of the system—asking questions, nurturing, connecting, reversing, and more—in order to paint the picture of *their* pain. During the conference call I mentioned earlier, the one involving the president of Network, Inc., he asked the adversary, "*How* do you think this problem can be solved?" An interrogative-led question, of course. In the end, the other company offered to pay Network an additional $200,000 per machine: $100,000 to reach breakeven, $100,000 for profit. Moreover, they proposed to grant—not loan, but simply give—Network several million dollars in order to ensure its financial stability.

Sound too good to be true? Maybe, but it is true. Apparently the Network president's presentation had given the adversary a clear picture of current and future pain if they didn't get those machines! But my client didn't accept this offer immediately. After four more meetings, they secured additional orders for more machines. Bottom line: Network had an immediate turn-around on the bottom line of tens of millions of dollars and then secured $100 million in new orders. The switch from the old sales team to the new one took about a year and a half. The new team of seven people produced—and is still producing—about three times the dollar volume generated by the old team of thirty people.

What better example could we find of the rule that the value of any negotiation—the price that will be paid in any negotiation—is directly related to the clarity of the vision of pain? What better example of the rule that the greater the pain, the higher the price the adversary will pay to have it made better or taken away? (Now, how could the win-win paradigm have worked for beleaguered Network? It couldn't have. How in the world could the same lame negotiating style that had gotten them into this bind have gotten them out of it? Impossible.)

Sometimes, one simple question can create a vision of the pain and quickly drive a decision. Recall the negotiation between my client and the doctors at the hospital regarding whether his baby girl would be transferred to the other hospital for surgery. My client thought this transfer was too risky. He and his wife wanted the doctors from the other hospital to perform the op-eration in the hospital where their baby already was. My client asked only one question of the head of the neonatal unit: *How much risk are you willing to take with my child's life?*

After the father asked his interrogative-led question, the doc-tor considered his answer carefully. The question about the baby's pain was designed to make the doctor think about his own pain: *How much risk am I willing to take to transfer this baby?* To his great credit, the doctor did not shoot from the hip, know-it-all style. And though he knew nothing about my system of negotiating, he did understand that he had so far failed to paint a clear picture of my *client's* own pain in this situation. The doctor replied calmly that yes, there was risk in transferring the baby, and yes, there was an operating theater at this hospital, and yes, they could request the specialists from the other hospital to come over here. But, he continued, the *real* risk for my client's daughter was not what happened during the operation, but post-op complications. If the baby was moved to the other hospital, she would have the best care available to her within seconds should an emergency arise after the operation. If she remained in her current hospital, the best care was phone calls, beepers, pagers, and urgent car trips away.

Now the pain on both sides was very clear. My client immediately changed his mind and okayed the transfer to the other hospital. The operation was successful, and the baby is now a perfectly healthy toddler.

Painting the Pain Is an Art

"Your greatest strength is your greatest weakness." I quote these words from Emerson for the second time, because truer words were never written. For a negotiator, they're pure gold. The naturally glib negotiator talks too much. The brilliant negotiator tries to overpower his adversary with intelligence. The friendly, compassionate negotiator tries to "save" his adversary. The aggressive negotiator tries to browbeat his adversary. The list of scenarios goes on and on and on, and the painting of pain is one area in which the serious negotiator must be particularly careful not to get carried away with his or her particular strength and skill. You want to avoid that emotional pendulum I wrote about in the section on strip lines in chapter 7. You want to avoid the too positive and the too negative. The vision has to be clear, but so does the solution you offer. You must not frighten or anger the adversary, you can't appear to be lording it over your adversary, you must nurture at all times. Painting the pain is one of the real arts of negotiation. You must wield the brush with the touch of an Old Master.

10

The Real Budget and How to Build It

The Importance of Time, Energy, Money, and Emotion

KIDS PLAYING BASEBALL are great—a textbook in human psychology. What happens when youngsters hit a ground ball? First, they run toward first base. (Or sometimes they head for third base, but let's assume they do run in the right direction.) What *else* is happening? Often, they look over at the coach for approval, then watch the ball, then look as the shortstop catches the ball, then watch the throw. The trained Little Leaguers would duck their heads and run full speed to first base, concentrating on the base. This is the proper behavioral goal, but kids usually don't do this. By watching the action in the field, they run more slowly and greatly increase the chance that the ball will beat them to the bag. And often the runner's fear of making an out takes over. The kid slows down or even quits running and looks at the coach again, thinking the throw will be in time, forgetting that the first baseman may drop the ball—quite possible—or be pulled off the bag by a high or wide throw—*very* possible. In short, the hitter's behavior and activity are not disciplined and proper habits have not been developed. That run to first base is not "valid."

Kids are kids. They say and do the darnedest things. What's really amazing is that we adults exhibit the same failing. When I was a youngster my whole family enjoyed watching an old game show called *Beat the Clock,* with Bob Collyer as the host. He was the Regis Philbin of that era, I guess. The idea of the show was that contestants ran around the studio trying to beat the clock in the accomplishment of some ridiculous task. For some strange reason, I got to thinking about *Beat the Clock* years later, and I realized that we, the audience, focused on the clock, while we should have been watching the contestants' activity and behavior. Worse, the *contestants* were always looking up to see how much time they had remaining. But this shouldn't have mattered. They were working as fast as they could, weren't they? If they beat the clock, they beat it; if they didn't, they didn't. Watching the clock only slowed them down and made it more likely that they would not beat the clock. Bottom line: usually it wasn't the clock that beat them. They beat themselves with what I call invalid behavior.

I've seen such self-defeating behavior on the other side of the table so many times it's ridiculous. Nine times out of ten—ninety-nine out of one hundred, I'm tempted to say—unsuccessful negotiators have beat themselves. It has been said that my entire system is set up as a guide to behavior, and I don't quarrel with this assessment. The fuels of the system are certainly guides to behavior—specific, concrete *dos* and *do nots,* right down to choosing which words you should use when asking questions. And being unokay, not needing, blank slating, painting pain—these are all principles of valid behavior. The subject of this chapter—budget—is another principle directed at the same purpose.

As with pain, "budget" in my system is almost a technical term. It is much more than your normal budget, much more than an itemization of projected costs, because the *real* price to be paid in the negotiation goes way beyond dollars and cents. Budget in the Camp System breaks down into three budgets that help us account for and control this *real* price in time-and-energy, money, and emotional investment. (I unite time and energy because it's hard to spend one without spending the other as well.) The overall budget is a comprehensive, powerful tool, another means by which we can retain control in the negotiation by making certain that our investments are working for us, not against us.

Only the money budget is numerical. The other two employ a different kind of assessment, but one that we can keep up with quite accurately. My rough-and-ready formula for calculating the *overall* budget for a negotiation gives "time" a value of x, "energy" $2x$, "money" $3x$, and "emotion" $4x$. Obviously, these are not empirically based numbers. They're a way to drive home the point of *relative* importance. If you are spending only time and energy in a negotiation, you have a budget of $1x \times 2x$, for a total budget of $2x$. If you start throwing real money around, your budget is $2x \times 3x$, or $6x$. The *real* budget has tripled over the budget for time-and-energy alone. What happens if your *emotions* enter the negotiation and the equation in a powerful way? Multiply that $6x$ by $4x$. You're up to $24x$, a large relative number that serves mainly to demonstrate how important the budget for emotion is, how dangerous emotional investment is.

To repeat, budget is the way you keep on top of the *real* price to be paid in the negotiation, which goes way beyond dollars and cents. Both sides in a negotiation have a budget for each of the three categories, and your job is to make certain that you know both yours *and* your adversary's. Budget is a warning, in effect, to take careful account of factors that are usually overlooked in a negotiation and to realize their importance. And it's a way to help you use these factors to your advantage in a negotiation. Needless to say, we want to keep our own budgets as low as possible while reaping the benefit of the adversary's higher budgets.

At all times, the real price we are prepared to pay is regulated by effective decision making based on our mission and purpose and on our vision of the negotiation. The danger is that we become overinvested in a negotiation and our decision making goes out of whack. We start thinking in such terms as *Well, we've already invested so much in this deal, we have to get something out of it.* That's the classic logic that yields bad deals. It's the kind of logic that seduces us into egregiously violating our mission and purpose. I don't know of a better example of what can happen when we let our sense of a max'ed-out budget affect our enforcement of mission and purpose than NASA's decisions prior to the *Challenger* tragedy. The agency knew about the O-ring problem, but its budget for the space shuttle project was already so high that it compromised its values, its mission and purpose, and its people.

The *Challenger* disaster was a human tragedy. You'll be dealing with situations of less import, thank goodness, but bad decision making from budgets gone awry is what we want to avoid by knowing and setting budgets in the first place.

The Time-and-Energy Budget

When was the last time someone asked, "May I have a few minutes of your time?" and you granted this person the time? This was basic courtesy, but by doing so you unwittingly placed little or no value on those minutes, correct? And if enough such unsolicited, unwanted, time-eating episodes pile up in the day—answering e-mail may come to mind for many of us; it does for me—a considerable amount of time is down the drain by day's end. Professional negotiators must carefully consider the value of our time, but usually this calculation just doesn't enter our minds.

> *"By signing this application, all you are doing is making an application, and once it's been approved you can decide if you want the policy. Of course this doesn't mean you are committed, it only means you are making application."*
>
> *"Okay, fine."*
>
> *"I'll call to tell you when your doctor's appointment is scheduled for your physical. It won't take long, you'll be in and out of there in no time."*
>
> *"Well, I'm going to be pretty busy for the next few weeks. Call me, and we'll see if we can work it out."*

And the chase is on for this life insurance salesman. How many calls will it take to get the adversary to the doctor? How much work goes into application preparation and underwriting? The salesman must think about this. To the untrained negotiator, time is a virtually free commodity given away right and left, so he ends up spending his commission, in effect, in time-and-energy.

Do we really have much "time to spare"? No. Warren Buffett may have all the *money* in the world, but he doesn't have any more *time* than you and I do. And believe me, Warren Buffett understands this. I don't imagine he hands out appointments right and left. In any negotiation, the calculation of time *must* enter our minds, because the time at our disposal and at our adversary's disposal is so fleeting and so finite. Maybe we don't like to focus on the limited hours of the day because we don't like to focus on the limited days of our lives. Maybe that's it, I don't know, but I do know that as negotiators we must train ourselves to care about the hours of the day. We must understand that time can be used against us in many ways, especially as a way to increase the real price of a negotiation and eventually bring about a possible compromise. All of a sudden we're saying to ourselves, "I've got too much time in this. I can't turn away now."

For the crafty negotiator, increasing the adversary's time budget is the oldest game in the book: making you wait an hour, flooding you with e-mails and faxes, asking you to drive two hours or fly eight hours, canceling at the last minute—or arguing for nine months about the shape of the negotiating table, which is what Ho Chi Minh's team did in the 1974 Paris peace negotiations, driving up Nixon and Kissinger's time budget. The North Vietnamese had all the time in the world for this negotiation—after all, they'd already been fighting France or us for a generation—and they knew that Nixon and Kissinger did not.

Such budget-building ploys are transparent. Others are not. The use of time against you can start with something as common as your trying to get an appointment.

"Just give me ten minutes and let me show you what I've got, Sara."
"Okay, when?"

You've got the appointment! Your company has been trying for years to open the golden door, and you've finally succeeded. But then your adversary is a no-show. You're stood up—no explanation, no phone call, no insincere apology. The untrained negotiator now crashes, thinking that valuable time has been wasted.

But what if Sara *keeps* the appointment? Look how she can still use time against you: "Okay, show me what you've got. But remember, I have to leave soon." The untrained negotiator gets excited and starts talking and spills every feature and benefit of his position, thinking, *I'm really getting my money's worth out of these ten minutes!*

No, he's not. The adversary is getting *her* money's worth out of these ten minutes, because she's finding out everything she wants to know. Meanwhile, the untrained negotiator isn't finding out anything. He's violating every rule in my system. He's out of control—not asking good questions, not blank slating, not living in the adversary's world. And he *is* trying to close this deal today. He is chasing time, as I like to put it.

"Just a little more time and they'll buy!"

Nothing could be further from the truth. Never chase time.

For the man or woman in straight sales, conventional wisdom tells you just to get out there and make proposals, get in front of people and spill your guts, then ask them to buy. In effect, play a numbers game. Make up for self-defeating behavior with raw numbers. A hundred lines in the water must be better than five. Okay, you may catch a few small fry this way, if you have the energy and the self-image to withstand the pounding (recommended viewing: *Death of a Salesman,* the Lee J. Cobb performance), but you will never come close to your full potential. Why throw up a three-pointer with two defenders hanging all over you? Why throw a long pass into two-man coverage downfield? Why swing at pitches that aren't in the strike zone? Why try to carry the lake at 220 yards? Why drive to an appointment an hour away without knowing your chances for valid negotiation are good?

In the discussion about warm calls versus cold calls in chapter 1, when I was warning about the danger of the former and the surprising benefit of the latter, I was dealing with telephone calls. Never drive around town on cold calls. The great negotiator in any field won't walk next door, much less get in her car or on the airplane, without a clear picture of the negotiation coming up—a clear picture of the adversary's pain and a firm knowledge that the adversary has the budgets in time-and-energy, money, and emotion to pay—negotiate—to have this pain taken away. This is the only *valid* appointment for the man or woman in straight sales, and the rule applies just as stringently to corporate and all other negotiators, no matter what the field.

It also applies to advertising. The following paragraph on that subject may seem like a digression, but I think not. I think it drives home the point about valid appointments—of any sort—very well. Every morning, all of us wake up to advertising: in the newspaper, surfing the Web, on television, in the mail, on the radio, on the billboards, on the magazine jackets in the airplane, on the ticket jackets for the airline, on paper coffee cups. Advertising is literally everywhere. It is certainly one of our greatest commercial strengths in the United States. But how should you use advertising to do business? I once had a student who had one hundred thousand coupons delivered to homes each month, costing a nickel a coupon, $60,000 per year. He earned from $225,000 to $360,000, gross revenue, from those coupons. Then an advertising rep presented him with a campaign to cut his advertising budget in half, using the newspaper instead of coupons.

When my student asked my advice I asked a question of my own—several of them, in fact (and interrogative-led, naturally, since I was trying to build his vision). "What is the circulation of the local paper?" I asked. He didn't know, but soon found out it was sixty-eight thousand.

"Who are you selling to?"

"Jim, that's easy. Working families who own their own homes."

"How many working families get the newspaper each day at home?"

He didn't know, but even if every subscriber to the newspaper was a working-class homeowner, the total was sixty-eight thousand, considerably fewer than the one hundred thousand coupons he put in circulation.

"When you are at work, do you buy from newspaper advertising?"

"Well, come to think of it, no, I don't."

"What do you think you should do?"

"Maybe I need to do more research, and maybe I had better not cut out the coupon campaign."

I recommend David Ogilvy's book *Ogilvy on Advertising*. It's all there. The principles of advertising as a sales prospecting tool are simple, and they pertain to many of the negotiations we're discussing in this book as well. No matter how good an appointment or meeting looks or sounds at first blush, it must meet the criteria of validity. If it doesn't offer the prospect of producing results you can measure, it has to go. Let me just repeat what I said earlier: The great negotiator in any field must not lift a finger without a clear picture of the negotiation coming up—a clear picture of the adversary's pain and a firm knowledge that the adversary has the budgets in time-and-energy, money, and emotion to pay—negotiate—to have this pain taken away. You will be able to uncover budget easily when you come to understand, from trial and error, the risk to the negotiation if budget isn't solidly understood and in the open. This doesn't mean that your adversary will necessarily tell you straight out about their budgets (although he might, unthinkingly). Mainly, you'll learn to discover budget as your adversary shares his vision of his pain. The higher the pain, the higher the budget. People will pay a much higher price than you would ever ask.

"Bill, what would you budget to solve this problem?"

"John, I'm not sure what it takes in dollars and cents, but with your help we will build the necessary budget."

I'm not saying that every appointment or meeting must pan out or make progress or it becomes, in retrospect, invalid. Not at all. You have no control over that ultimate result. I've already related the story of my clients who flew to Ireland and were stood up. That was nevertheless a perfectly valid meeting within the ongoing negotiation. Being stood up is annoying, but it happens, and it's not the end of the world. It becomes a problem only if you crash emotionally and thereby concede leverage in the negotiation to your adversary. As I've mentioned, my stood-up clients got back on the next flight home from Ireland and, a couple of days later, wrote a calm letter suggesting a meeting over here the next time. And they got it.

When stood up by anyone, the trained negotiator should calmly sit back and figure out whether he'd like to try again or just fade away. He should, in short, consult his budget for time-and-energy. This is not a specific number of hours, in all likelihood, although it could be. It is a sense, an assessment, a *judgment* based on experience. It is, most of all, an *awareness* that your time-and-energy is not free. The negotiator needs to remember that the adversary's budget is going up right along with his own.

Patience, my friend, always patience. That's the watchword. When someone tries to drive time up on you, regardless of how, patience will be your sword. And with a solid mission and purpose in place, he or she won't be able to drive up time. By definition, your mission and purpose is a long-term aim, a continuing task and responsibility. Therefore, time actually becomes your ally; it is there to work for you, not to run out on you. Budgeting time is a matter of disciplining ourselves, of maintaining patience, of following our mission and purpose with dedication and skill. If these are handled well, the time-on-the-calendar question takes care of itself.

Time can be wasted in a one-hour negotiation. It can be utilized to the fullest in a one-year negotiation. Time spent tells us nothing either way about time *well* spent.

When people try to drive up your budget by putting deadlines in place, even if it's only a ten-minute time limit for a presentation, with patience and a mission and purpose, you can eagerly embrace such a deadline and craft your presentation accordingly. Every minute of *your* time in a negotiation is a minute of *their* time as well. Two can play that game.

"Bill, what day are you looking at on your calendar?"
"Well, John, this is a real problem. Could you make it today?"
*"Bill, I can't get there until tomorrow. What time would be best
for you?"*

If you are using time well, you are always building your adversary's budget. You can build it with canceled meetings of
your own, with "urgent" phone calls that you don't return immediately, by not leaving detailed messages that might save the
adversary time but cost you time—or even by putting your
adversary on hold for fifteen seconds. I'm thinking of one
particular episode when I mention that last scenario. In a six-
month-long negotiation, a client received a call from the adversary, who wanted to review a letter my client had sent him. Even
though the letter was on my client's desk, staring him in the face,
he told the adversary he'd have to put him on hold and go look
for the letter. Only fifteen seconds, but if you're worried about
an issue, fifteen seconds is long enough for all kinds of thoughts
to race through your mind. Meanwhile, those brief seconds gave
my client time to collect and calm himself for the discussion to
follow. My client was also making a subtle statement that he was
not needy here, that he didn't even have the letter in front of
him.

Is building the adversary's budget just silly gamesmanship?
Not at all. It's a valuable way to get your opponent's attention, to
push their vision of their pain. Adversaries dally, play games of
their own, and in many other ways simply aren't serious. These
folks need your help in order to push forward to serious decision
making. One way you do this is by building their budgets, which
then focus the attention marvelously. Ho Chi Minh just kept

building and building and *building* the Americans' time budget in
Vietnam until we finally figured out that the war was never
going away. Think about it: building our time budget was the
best way the North Vietnamese had to get us to see the ultimate
pain of our position, which was that this war was never going
away.

No, building budgets definitely is not gamesmanship. It's inte-
gral to painting the pain for the adversary and getting the adversary to get a clear vision as quickly as possible. In a phrase, *time
intensifies pain*. As the investment of time mounts higher and
higher, so does the psychological pressure. Many negotiators
allow themselves to get the sense that they're under a deadline,
beyond which they've "wasted their time." My clients love to
hear from the other side, "Okay, let's cut to the chase," because
this may mean that the time-and-energy budget for the adversary is reaching its allotted total, and that they are seeing the pain
very, very clearly, and they're finally just about willing and able
to make an effective decision.

For your own part, make certain that you do have "all the
time in the world"—and if you don't, be ready to walk away.
Remember, you only want this deal, you do not need this deal.
They may now need this deal. Crucial difference. (As I've said, in
a negotiation between two Camp-System adversaries, there's little need for budget-building tactics, because both parties are
trained to move quickly to the essential issues, the essential vision, the essential pain, the essential decisions.)

All time is energy, of course, but in tough negotiations there
may be energy spent beyond time. The work of negotiating is
draining, and we really don't have any energy to waste. We want
it to be there for us when we can use it the most. Never under-

estimate the energy that's going to be required to do a deal. Keeping our needs in check and completing the activity and behavioral goals we set will help us conserve our own energy and waste theirs. Invalid, pointless appointments and meetings? A waste of energy. Accepting "maybe" for an answer? A waste of energy. Accepting "yes" for an answer? A waste of energy. Asking questions that don't do you any good? A waste of energy. Failing to blank slate, making assumptions instead of doing valid research? A waste of energy. *Needing* something? A terrible waste of energy.

On the other hand, the old adage "Penny-wise, pound-foolish" is right on. We *do* want to spend energy in preparation and research, but the shocking reality is that many people won't or don't prepare for negotiations. They won't spend the time or the energy required. This isn't conserving energy, this is laziness, which inevitably wastes energy at a later stage of the negotiation. As I've said, my clients are often shocked by the poor preparation of some Fortune 100 companies.

My system can be described as nothing more or less than a way to behave in negotiations, but it can also be looked at as a way to save energy. If our energy is wasted, it is of our own doing. We cannot blame the adversary, because we are in control of our own behavior. Most well-trained adversaries will try to use energy against you, whether they would put their actions in these terms or not. But if you're stood up, for example, exactly how much energy over and above the time that's wasted *is* under your control? And you can respond in kind, of course. Build their energy budget. Increase the preparation required by the adversary to complete the deal ("This just doesn't make sense to us. Can you redo it?"). Tactically withhold decision makers from the negotiation ("We've talked this over and decided that your team needs to go to New York to show this to Mr. Smith"). Always be guided by your mission and purpose.

Be aware of personal health and stamina. Know your endurance limits. Don't get caught short of energy with jet lag. Regular physical exercise is important. Don't allow yourself to be locked away during negotiations. Take breaks and walks to keep the energy up and the head clear. Alcohol can steal your energy; beware of social gatherings combined with business.

How many times have you read about a big labor conflict that was finally resolved at four in the morning? That's because when we get tired, we become impatient and more vulnerable. After days, weeks, maybe months of negotiations, all sides finally decide to stay with it until they have a deal, each trying to wear down the other side. The physically stronger, more energetic side gets the best of the deal. Any marathon negotiation turns into a contest of endurance, plain and simple. You must know your own endurance and not hesitate to call a time-out, whether you're in an hour-long meeting or a round-the-clock negotiation.

The Money Budget

"Put your money where your mouth is." It always seems to come down to money, doesn't it? Or as some wise person once said, "When they say it's not about money, *it's about money*." Once you and your adversary start spending real money during the negotiation and get serious about exchanging much more when the deal is signed, the value of any negotiation goes up dramatically. Remember, time is 1*x,* energy 2*x,* and money 3*x,* roughly and relatively speaking.

The value of anything goes up when money is involved. Who is more likely to attend and get the most out of seminars or classes, the student who works from midnight to four in the morning to pay her fees, or the student on the athletic scholarship, with free tutors and five years to finish at no cost at all? Who's more likely to work at the new negotiation system, the student who pays his way because he's genuinely interested and ambitious, or the employee sent by her boss? I know that answer, and so do you.

Within the context of a negotiation, money is a surprisingly slippery commodity. Any given sum means different things to different people. On the most obvious level, an unexpected $1,000 expense affects the clerk earning $20,000 far differently than it affects the executive earning $120,000, and it registers differently with each of them. Less obviously, perhaps, a consumer may not be able to see value if the price of a given product is too *low* in his frame of reference. On the other hand, he will search for value if the price is deemed high. A classic case is Callaway's Big Bertha golf club. Ely Callaway intentionally jacked up the price of this club when he first introduced it years ago, setting it far above the industry standard and far above what he needed to make a good profit. As a marketing man, he understood that at a lower price, the Big Bertha would have been just another golf club, and the well-heeled target market wouldn't have been able to see the value. But the $400 driver (initially; even more now) caught the attention of golfers, who then searched for value—and found it, as any golfer who has tried the club will attest. The Big Bertha changed the industry.

Just as with time-and-energy, you want money to work for you and against your adversary. You will try to drive up your adversary's budget by making the negotiation literally expensive, and your adversary will try to do the same, because everyone knows that a money squeeze is often followed by compromise if the untrained negotiator loses sight of his mission and purpose. You have to know your actual dollars-and-cents budget for this negotiation, and you have to have a sense for their dollars-and-sense budget and a sense of how they stand financially. What is your adversary's frame of reference? What's real money to them?

If you are constrained by money and your adversary is not, watch out. I guess the most obvious example of this situation is a lawsuit between a lawyer representing a single client against a large corporation. Legal proceedings are not, technically speaking, negotiations, since they're regulated by legal factors that don't affect true negotiations, but my point stands: The corporation is in a position to drive up the independent lawyer's dollars-and-cents budget past the point of endurance, whereas the lawyer does not have this capability. It's not a fair fight, in this regard. (I say this without taking a position on the controversial subject of torts litigation.) Therefore some consumer-products companies have a policy of refusing to settle lawsuits. They'll spend $100,000 in legal fees instead of settling for $20,000, figuring that this announced policy keeps the suits to a minimum and saves money in the long run. I'll bet they're right.

In any event, if you're a lawyer you'd want to know about this policy beforehand, wouldn't you? Do your research. If you're negotiating with a big multinational, wouldn't you want to know that they have the habit of driving up money budgets by insisting on meetings all over the country, and often the world? This tactic of driving up the dollars-and-cents budget of their smaller suppliers is basic strategy for the purchasing departments of the big multinationals. It works to perfection against win-

win, of course, but the supplier who's using the Camp System doesn't lie to himself about the situation. He just sees it clearly, sets the money budget, and is prepared to lose *every dollar* of it. In this way, the supplier protects himself from *needing* and from compromise as the crunch approaches.

The professional negotiator engages in an ongoing assessment of the money budget at all times. If you don't have enough cash reserves for the long haul, your negotiation is, for all intents and purposes, over with before it even gets going. So don't even get going. Seek your deals elsewhere. The four Camp clients who flew to Ireland for a meeting, where they were promptly stood up, "lost" $20,000, but the money was in their budget and they had no expectations.

How's this for trying to drive up the budget? My client was ready to ship two systems to their biggest customer, a giant multinational. These were special-order systems—state-of-the-art work worth several million dollars apiece—with hard P.O.'s, and when the customer's truck backed up to the loading dock my client was ready to roll out the machines. Imagine their surprise when the truck driver announced that he had specific orders not to pick up the two main systems. He had been authorized to pick up only another subsidiary component. That's hardball for you. The multinational was hoping to get a *literally* last-minute discount. But two can play that game. On the telephone, then and there, with the truck driver waiting, officers with my client took an aggressive stand, reminding high officers with the multinational that this was a confirmed deal based on a long negotiation, and stating clearly that they needed a "ship in place" letter. This is a legal document that gives one party the right, for accounting purposes, to move an asset off the books of one company and onto the books of another. My client got that ship in place letter, because they were entitled to it.

Some years back, I was introduced to a young man named Craig Lehmkuhl. Craig had just left the building industry as a contractor in order to join the real estate industry as a commercial broker. He had a family, and, like many young family men, he had very little money. But he was committed to training in negotiation. Craig was scraping the bottom to pay for his training and, as he told me later, "I wasn't about to waste my money by not applying the system." My newest client got his big break three months into our work when he had the opportunity to earn a substantial six-figure commission. During our coaching sessions and system studies, Craig had never missed a beat. He learned by leaps and bounds, but it was not until the last negotiation session with his adversary in this deal that he learned just what the value of money means to a negotiation: everything. In the bitter end, money is the toughest business decision.

I'll let Craig tell his own story:

"I had spent a lot of time working on this deal, including a trip to the lender in Southern California. That was valuable, but the airfare alone was more than I could afford. All in all, I was reaching my budget, and my emotions seemed out of control. This was the biggest deal of my life. If I pulled this off, I would make more than I made in all my working life. But in Southern California the closing agent informed me I was $50,000 short. Try as I might, I had no way of throwing this sum of money into the pot. I saw my commission going right down the toilet. I didn't think we had a chance of doing the deal. I couldn't see the seller putting in any more money.

"I had a problem. Actually, I had two problems. First, I didn't understand the price of this negotiation to the seller, and second, I

couldn't see him writing a $50,000 check. So with my heart jammed into my throat I returned to the seller and told him, in my most not-okay way, that two major problems had killed the deal. First, the deal was $50,000 short. Second, I didn't have the heart to ask him to throw in more money. His $200,000 contribution had moved the deal this far, and I couldn't ask him to throw in an extra $50,000, could I? What happened next was amazing. It happened so quickly. He simply asked me if another $50,000 would really close the deal? I was so emotional I didn't even realize he had asked the question. I just said yes. He didn't blink an eye, just opened his desk, took out a large checkbook, and handed the check to me with a smile and said he was very happy. He had been prepared to write a much larger check! He explained that his losses could have been much greater. He'd invested so much in this negotiation, he just wasn't going to lose this deal. I was shocked. It hit me like a ton of bricks. The money he had already spent made the negotiation so valuable he couldn't let it go away."

You must know your own budget for money and, as Craig learned, you must know your adversary's budget as well.

Quite a few years ago, one of my very best students was conducting what was shaping up as the largest negotiation in the history of his company. At that time, the largest negotiated deal to date had been $1.2 million. This deal might come in at something over $9 million. It would be difficult, but the company's decision makers determined that there were adequate resources to take on such a large project and the negotiation it would entail. Given the green light, this young man burned the midnight oil structuring his mission and purpose, his goals and objectives. Picture yourself in his situation. You struggle and lose sleep. Your life becomes more intense. Your commitment to the proj-

ect grows, and soon the boss is putting the fate of the company
in your hands: "We're counting on you, you're the guy, you're
the man, the only one who can pull this off." As the energy and
time escalate in this negotiation, problems arise. Colleagues are
getting in the way. If you are successful in closing the deal,
they'll be under a great deal of additional pressure to perform in
their jobs. They say they want you to win, but they are also
afraid you will. You need their support, and they pledge to be
there, but the work you ask of them comes in late or poorly
done or not at all. Now you're afraid to let anyone else get involved. You're beginning to feel very alone. Your own budget
for time-and-energy is getting high. But you must continue.
Even under all these pressures, the energy you have already
spent is also the energy driving you forward. You do a great job
negotiating—eighty different mini-agendas in all (the subject of
chapter 12), well over a dozen solid presentations to various
teams of adversaries, a firm and welcome "no" heard at least ten
times. You can smell victory. You are prepared to make what you
hope will be the final presentation—and then the boss says he's
awfully proud of you, but he has decided to take over the negotiation himself.

The man in the corner office is stepping in, and you won't be
needed any longer. Unbelievable, but what can you do? What
do you feel? Relief? Not a chance: You're a player. Disappointment? Worse: You're mad as hell. You've set the whole thing up,
and now he'll probably lose the deal. He's not a trained negotiator.

Predictably, the untrained boss's presentation is a joke and
a disaster. He doesn't know the system established by his
negotiator—you—and he ignores the one briefing he gets from
you. His presentation of features and benefits is beside the point

and of no interest to the other side. He makes everyone on the adversary's board who's sitting in on the presentation feel unokay. And guess what happens? He is called the day after the presentation and told that the adversary has no interest in his company's providing the required services. It's over.

What did my client do now, in real life? He kept negotiating. He didn't quit. He didn't yell. Quite simply, he controlled his emotions and *stayed in the system*. The adversary may have been disgusted with his boss, but the deal wasn't dead. He knew this, because he knew that while he had spent a great deal of time and energy and money, the total price was still within the budget. Just as important, he knew that the budget for his adversary was *also* very high by this time. He knew their pain intimately. He made the calls, he wrote the letters to bring everyone back to the table—and he soon closed the deal.

And who tried to take all the credit in the end? Who else?

The moral of this story: If you know the price and manage your time and energy and money and stay within budget and serve your mission and purpose, you're okay regardless of what the boss does.

The Emotion Budget

The thrill of victory! The agony of defeat! I'll bet you recognize those words almost immediately, because they have become clichés in our culture, thanks to ABC's *Wide World of Sports*. I still remember the ski jumper whose goggles fly off as he crashes over the side of the ski jump and the American hockey team celebrating their unbelievable victory over the Soviet squad, back in 1980 when the United States and the USSR were bitter adversaries. And when it comes to my son's college football games, I know all about thrill and agony. For sports fans, these extreme emotions are fine. They're mandatory for the fun. For negotiators, they're dangerous.

I'll stick by my original calculus: time is $1x$, energy is $2x$, money $3x$, and emotion $4x$. Emotions have an *extremely* high value in any negotiation. The value of the negotiation increases by many multiples when emotional pain or excitement is invested. The reason money is the toughest business decision is that money issues are *also* emotional issues for most of us. I guess there are people who don't care about money, but will you find them in the business world?

The excitement of winning and the pain of losing, of failing, are the two key emotions for both you and your adversary, and sophisticated corporate negotiating teams are trained to drive up your emotional budget—as well as the other two budgets, of course—with promises, threats, ridiculous requests and deadlines, sudden exclamations that the deal has gone south, and the like. But you must control your needs, your positive and negative expectations, your fears, your ego, your responses, and your decisions. You must not expect to manage the actual wins or losses, because you can't do this. You can only manage the means to the end: stay within your system, manage your activity, manage your behavior. This is all the armor you need. At the same time, you build needs, expectations, fears, and egos in the adversary in order to increase the value of the negotiation for him.

Know your budget. *Control* your budget. Know their budget. *Build* their budget. These rules apply for time-and-energy, for money, for emotions. When you master them, you really can't fail.

11

The Shell Game

Be Sure You Know the
Real *Decision Makers*

WHO'S CALLING THE shots? Who are the real decision makers within the adversary's bureaucracy? This might seem, at first glance, to be a fairly mundane issue, but it's not. It is a critically important issue in any negotiation, even though you can read book after book on the subject and never find a single acknowledgment that the question of who's calling the shots demands immediate attention. How can you create vision and paint the pain effectively without knowing who the decision makers for the adversary really are? You can't, so the decision-making process within your adversary's organization must be discovered and understood at the very beginning of the negotiation, or as soon thereafter as possible. If you don't accomplish this, you drive up your time-and-energy budget, maybe your money budget, and, if you're not careful, your emotion budget.

As a rule, the bigger the organization the more complex and confusing the decision-making process can be. When you're dealing with a big multinational, as some of my clients do, solving the shell game can be as frustrating as any aspect of the negotiation. In fact, you will encounter adversaries who play the shell game for just this purpose—to drive up your budget. Now the decision making is here, now it's there, now it's elsewhere.

When was the last time you heard, "Just show me and I'll take it to the board"? Or, "If I like it, I'll recommend it, and they always stamp my recommendations. It's just a formality. Just put your bid together based on the specs and I'll do the rest." But it seldom works out this way, does it? When you stop to think about it, the situation couldn't be this easy. Think of the number of times you as an individual were, in theory, the sole decision maker regarding a problem, but in the end asked the opinion and approval of someone else. We do this all the time. In my own family, the loyal dog seems to call the shots much of the time. It is no different for our adversaries. Many times, the adversary does not even know its *own* decision process as it directly concerns your negotiation. You will have to help them figure it out.

Some experts specialize in analyzing how decision making differs culturally around the world. In the United States we supposedly have a vertical process, while in Japan it's horizontal. I believe that most decision-making structures have both elements, and many surprising twists and turns as well. In my seminars I sometimes tell the story about the attempted change in the daily training regimen of a major college athletic department. It turned out that this change affected the schedule of the janitorial staff. In fact, the janitorial staff wielded something of a veto over aspects of the schedule. At the least, they had to be brought into the loop. So you never know. But you *must* know.

I'll never forget the episode in which I learned the painful facts of life on this subject. This was back in the 1970s, when I recruited on the West Coast for the Ohio State football team. I was working for Woody Hayes, and I cannot tell you how proud I was to do so. We were interested in a wonderful young man and running back named Freeman McNeil, who played high school ball in Los Angeles. All the big football colleges were recruiting Freeman, and I was on this recruit 24/7, as we didn't say then but might say today. I talked with everyone imaginable: principal, teachers, coaches, family, everyone. Freeman's coach told me that the final decision would be made by Freeman and his family, with the coach's input. So far, so good. When I met Freeman himself, he said he was very interested in Ohio State, and he told me his decision would be based on his assessment of the school and Coach Hayes. Even better, because Woody Hayes was as impressive a man as I ever met. Everyone felt this way. This is a long story, so I'll cut some corners and jump to the weekend when Woody flew to California to meet Freeman. Everything went very well. I was so excited by that evening all I could see was Freeman scoring for Ohio State against USC in the Rose Bowl. Then Freeman's mother introduced us to her son's girlfriend, who told Woody and me that she and Freeman had been going steady two years. Coach Hayes immediately asked her where she was going to college. She replied, "Why, UCLA." In his most polite and nurturing tone the old man asked, "What will you study?" Again she answered with a radiant smile of perfect teeth, "Theater and drama."

The evening came to a triumphant end with my believing that Freeman McNeil was going to be the next Heisman Trophy winner for the Ohio State Buckeyes. I was slow. Coach Hayes wasn't. As we walked to the car he said to me, "Jim, you did a hell of a job with Freeman. You have put us in a great position here in California. But Freeman is going to UCLA. He would be better off with us, but he will decide on UCLA." I was flabbergasted. How did Woody know for sure? In response he asked me, "Jim, would you leave home to play for the Buckeyes?" Sure! "But would you leave your movie-star girlfriend alone at UCLA to play for the Buckeyes?" That's when I saw the light. I asked Woody when he had seen it, and he said, "Not until she said UCLA and theater. That's Hollywood, and that is hard to turn down. Freeman is being recruited by Hollywood and movie stars. He is a fine young man, but the most important part of his decision process is his girlfriend. Even he doesn't realize it. He thinks he is making the decision along with his mom and dad. He is, but his girl carries the most weight. She'll convince him to go to UCLA, and he'll never see it. If she wanted medicine, law, business, education, we could compete, but she is so damned pretty and she wants Hollywood."

I had not only failed to find *all* the decision makers, I had failed to find the *main* one. In the end, Freeman McNeil did go to UCLA, where he had a very good, if not Heisman Trophy, career. Then he was an All-Pro with the New York Jets and may someday be in the Professional Football Hall of Fame in Canton, Ohio.

That failure to find the decision maker was one mistake I never repeated during my days recruiting for Coach Hayes, but I have seen it committed umpteen times in business negotiations—by the adversary, not by the good guys. Recall the negotiation I described in chapter 9 between my client and the company it was trying to acquire, the one we finally resolved by building the monument to the founder, the widow's husband. With such an inflated price on the table and the negotiations going nowhere, I repeatedly asked the chief negotiator, "What the heck is driving this price?" He just didn't have a clue, and he's a really bright guy. He was convinced that the board of directors made the decisions, but I did my job as coach and went down with him the list of possible decision makers. Lawyers? No. Accountants? No. Heirs? Hmmmm. He hadn't thought about such potentially important shareholders. Who holds the largest block of stock and has most of the influence? He didn't know, but he'd find out. You know the rest of the story.

Why do negotiators often fail to find the real decision process? Why do many want to just get a decision, any decision, and get the heck out? One reason, I believe: They fear that they don't have the right behaviors to negotiate with the *real* decision makers. With my system, however, you do have those behaviors. In this intensely personal, emotionally fraught discovery of who really makes the decisions, your skills with nurturing, reversing, and 3+ will be key. With your mission and purpose in place, and using all your behavioral goals, and no matter how elaborate the decision-making process, you can handle it. You simply *negotiate* each piece of the puzzle until you have the information you need. It's just that simple (if arduous).

How do you find out the truth? The same way you find out the truth on any issue in a negotiation: You ask those interrogative-led questions.

"Of course you make the decisions. But who else might you want to talk with?"

"Who might be of service in making this decision?"

"Who should we invite to support your decision?"

"Who'd be sorry or upset if we left them out?"

"How will this decision be reached?"

"When will it be reached?"
"What criteria and paperwork must be in place for it to be reached?"

You need these answers. Eliminate all the wild cards you can think of. Continually ask yourself who's missing? Who's not in my loop who should be? And be ready for unearthing multiple decision makers, and be able and willing to negotiate with each and every one of them.

You'll Have to Deal with Blockers

In many, many instances, the biggest problem you'll encounter in this discovery process is someone on your adversary's team telling you, assuring you, promising you, guaranteeing you, that he is the decision maker when he's not. Why does this happen so often? Quite simply, this is yet another example of how we humans fight to be okay, and it's not okay to say, "I have to run everything past my branch manager." It's no exaggeration to state that the decision-making process in an organization is driven by people's need to feel okay. When we walk into a reception area, what is the receptionist fighting for? The feeling of being okay. It's human nature! Who wants to feel powerless? Our big businesses are divided into level after level after level: upper management, middle management, business development, engineering, legal, human resources—it's endless. We work in these big corporate environments, and often we feel like we're about to be swallowed up. We know we are replaceable, because we've seen the company plow ahead even if the CEO drops dead, but we want to *mean something* in this bigger scheme of things. We want to make a beneficial difference. We want to feel okay. And a key way we can do this is to insinuate ourselves into the decision-making process.

I call these sweet folks who want to play some kind of role "blockers." Beware of them. Once you have determined who the real decision makers are, it's often hard to get to them because of the blockers standing in the way. If you can't go around or over the blockers, you'll never get your deal. Remember my excellent student Craig Lehmkuhl from chapter 10, the guy who learned the anxious way that both sides in a negotiation have a budget. His adversary's was so high the man gladly wrote the check for $50,000. In the early days of Craig's work with me, his biggest problem was getting past the receptionists. This is the situation with lots of people in sales—and elsewhere. The blocker could be the receptionist who screens the calls, or the executive assistant, or the comanager, or, worst of all, the person you have incorrectly decided is the decision maker.

Do the blockers *think* of themselves as blockers? Sometimes yes, because they are under explicit instructions to block, but often no. They just know what makes them feel okay. They are by nature defensive and believe that their job description is to obstruct forward progress, to create obstacles, and ultimately to bring about your defeat. They may have other reasons for blocking as well. Their jobs might be on the line. They may be jealous, because you seem to be the decision maker for your company, while they obviously are not for their own; you're going to get a lot of credit or commissions or some kind of reward for this deal, while they're not. In short, what's in it for the blocker? Maybe not much.

Great leaders surround themselves with great blockers who love the game. You can count on this. Prepare for the person in a negotiation who loves the game. You could decide that the tangle of negative attitudes with a blocker may need to be put on the agenda with this person as "baggage." (I'm jumping the gun here and will explain this idea further in the next chapter.) But *always* show the blocker respect, even as you are circumventing her carefully guarded territory.

I have followed the travails of Network, Inc., the company that was in deep water with a terribly negotiated contract that they realized they simply couldn't honor. It would have put them out of business, so a new team of negotiators was called in—along with me. One of the first things we learned was that no one with Network knew who the real decision makers were on the other side. When they found out, they had never heard of a *single one* of these individuals. Now that's pretty amazing. As the new team nosed around and asked questions throughout the other company, the same three or four names kept popping up as candidates to be the real decision maker, but one other name was mentioned by everyone *except* those in this individual's division. This guy turned out to be where the buck stopped, and in his own division everyone blocked for him.

The first team of negotiators didn't know about him or anyone else of importance. They had been negotiating with blockers, plain and simple. They had been dealing with the purchasing office, and the purchasing office should never be in a negotiation. They handle the paperwork and not the decisions. Everyone knows this. The more power the old team gave to purchasing, the less effective they became. Once the new team came in, purchasing was for all intents and purposes out of the loop.

The second group of blockers that had to be dealt with by the new team were the technical evaluators of the machine in question. The head of this evaluation group had been displaced within his own company, as colleagues had been promoted all around him. He was standing still and didn't have a lot of positive feelings about where things stood. He was very defensive about every decision he had made in the past in the area in question, and he was doing everything he could to defend his decisions. Basic human nature. As it turned out, one of those decisions was responsible for almost $100 million worth of equipment sitting idly at his company. So he had a lot to defend, and the Network deal would make that equipment entirely obsolete. Everyone else in the department was now begging for the Network equipment, while the blocker was working as hard as he could to influence the decision makers otherwise. When this individual got wind of the fact that the new team from Network had finally found out who the real decision makers were, he immediately tried to sabotage any meeting between the parties, and the obstruction continued apace for the duration of that negotiation.

It Never Hurts to Start at the Top

You can get around your basic blocker in several ways. A surefire way is simply to start at the top. What happens if you start at the top? The top boots you down the ladder to the blocker, but this is fine because, presumably, you've been introduced into the blocker's territory with a stamp of approval. The blocker knows it's okay to talk to you, and the blocker knows that you know that he is indeed a blocker. Start at the top and you will be in a position to report to the top. You have a hall pass to the corner office upstairs. Blockers will therefore treat you with respect. If the CEO had time to talk to you, the blocker has time to talk to you. Or he had better find the time.

But all is not lost if you can't start at the top. You can still deal with the blocker from below.

> *Ring! Ring! "Hello, this is the office of the president of the United States. Tammy speaking."*
>
> *"Tammy, my name is Bill Jones and I need your help. What are the criteria I must meet to have an audience with the president? Tammy, who would have the ear of the president on matters of super-computers capable of putting billions of dollars into the Treasury without any additional taxes?"*
>
> *"Well, I recommend you speak with the chairman of the House Ways and Means Committee, Mr. Smith."*
>
> *"Tammy, do you know his most competent assistant I might talk to?"*
>
> *"Why yes, she's a classmate of mine, Betty. Would you like me to transfer you to her number?"*
>
> *"I'd appreciate that. Would you be so kind as to tell her why I am calling? It's very difficult to call out of the blue, as you know."*
>
> *"Yes, I'll be glad to do that. Let's see if we can reach her."*

A fantasy, yes, but this approach will get you somewhere. Don't just get around the blocker, but also get a useful introduction *from* the blocker. This is much easier to do when you understand what the blocker is really doing, which is trying to feel okay. Have a little sympathy. Engage in a little nurturing.

> *"Bill, I'd like to make a deal with you. I'd like to go over our proposal with you. If what I present to you is not acceptable and you know it won't fly, just tell me no, it won't fly, and I'll go away. Fair? Fair. That will be our deal. If you like what I propose and feel it is what the committee is looking for, all I ask is that you allow me to represent myself to the committee. Fair?"*

What have we done? We have protected our proposal and also protected Bill's okayness. If Bill accepts this proposal, he will fight for it, or at least strongly support your program to the committee. This approach usually works. If it doesn't, if Bill never allows anyone else to take a proposal to the committee, if he doesn't feel comfortable with you and is afraid the committee won't either, and will then blame him, you go to your second choice.

"Bill, I understand that under no circumstances will anyone but you talk to the committee. All I ask is if you don't like what I show you, just tell me no and I'll get out of your hair. But if you like our proposal and wish to recommend it to the committee, all I ask is that you let me coach you on my proposal and what you might say. Allow me to wait out in the hall, just in case there are any questions the committee wants answered. That way you are protected with adequate information in case something unexpected comes up. Fair? That will be our deal."

What if Bill won't accept this agenda? Go to your third choice for an agenda.

"Bill, I understand that no one is to be present during the committee meeting, even in the hall. All I ask is that you allow me to coach you on what to say, and if any question arises, allow me to wait in your office. You can call me there and I can provide you any information you need. Of course, if you don't like my proposal today, it's okay, you won't hurt my feelings. Just tell me no and I'll go away. We'll take a shot at working with you next time around."

If Bill still balks—unlikely, but possible—consult your time-and-energy budget, because this situation doesn't look promising. How much have you put into this negotiation? Are you fighting too hard? Are you *needy?* Should you simply walk away, no hard feelings? Whatever your decision, it will be a good one, because you have retained control of the negotiation. You have preserved the blocker's okayness. He's comfortable. You've given him every opportunity to say "no." You haven't tried to close him. You've given him every opportunity to create vision. And, finally, if you give up on Bill as a lost cause, you can always move in any other direction you like within the organization. The talented negotiator moves freely within the decision process. The talented negotiator enjoys solving the shell game.

12

Have an Agenda and Work It

Ride the Chaos Inherent
in Negotiation

M Y SYSTEM IS designed to help us control the chaos in a
negotiation—and sometimes "chaos" is not too strong a
word. Things get complicated quickly, and you can find yourself
being pushed and pulled by your adversaries in many different
directions. How many times have you found yourself wondering, *What just happened? What went wrong? What should I have
done differently? What should I do now? Who should I be talking to
and what should I say?* Bottom line: You're confused, you're flailing around, your budgets are out of control, and effective decision making is in jeopardy. Negotiating in this scattered, aimless
way is a good way to get your brains kicked in on a daily basis,
and that ain't fun. This chapter introduces that part of my system
that will tell you what went wrong, what to do next, how to
keep your negotiation on track, how to continue making effec-

tive decisions, how to keep your brains intact. The subject is agendas.

In all fields, the most successful people deal with the most difficult problems directly. Negotiation is no different. Your ability to identify the greatest problems and then to bring them into the negotiation head-on by way of an agenda will exponentially improve your record. Agendas also help us to maintain emotional control. They are our first line of defense in this regard, our surefire means of staying on track. I cannot overemphasize their value.

The preparation of the agenda is a terrific exercise in and of itself, as well as a test of your ability to see the negotiation clearly and to assign priorities. In a corporation with negotiating teams, valid agendas are absolutely crucial for keeping everyone on the team on the same page and talking with one voice, so to speak, in their various encounters with various adversaries. If five team members using the same agenda return with five drastically different answers from their counterpoints, they're well advised to stop and take a hard look at the discrepancies. Are the members of the other team not on the same page, or are they playing games? You need to know. For your part, if your team is having trouble crafting explicit agendas, you're also having trouble with mission and purpose, or with goals, or with blank slating, or with painting the pain, or with budgets, or with all of these.

As with mission and purpose and budgets, our Camp-System agendas are different from those used by most negotiators and businesspeople. The typical business agenda lists topics to be discussed, often in no particular order. Even if there is an order, we know what happens all too often: The anticipated order is more or less discarded and a free-for-all ensues. Like many other business meetings, this one ends up as a frustrating waste of time and energy. Our agendas must do better. They must provide a clear path through the negotiation thicket.

Every negotiating session—even a telephone call or an e-mail, no matter how short, even one minute or one paragraph— requires an agenda. Maybe this sounds radical at first, but it's really not. Every call and e-mail has some kind of purpose, doesn't it? I hope so. *So what's the purpose?* The agenda makes it clear. In fact, what can guide the day-to-day nuts and bolts of the negotiation *other than* agendas? You don't have to be a control freak to enjoy the control offered by agendas that really work.

Every Agenda Must Be Negotiated

"Joe, isn't this the greatest thing you've ever seen? Don't you need this right away? This is for you, Joe!"

Forget it. An adversary can never be asked to do something if a valid agenda was not negotiated.

"Bill, I said I would look at it, and I have. I never said I would act."

In my system, there are no hidden agendas. What would be the point of one? You hope to get a deal *that sticks in the end* by springing surprises? Hope again. The only agenda that is valid for purposes of negotiation—the only agenda that will produce results—is the one that has been negotiated with an adversary. Take a moment and be certain that you understand the implications of this rule: The only agenda that is valid for purposes of negotiation is the one that has been negotiated with the adversary. The more effective you are in negotiating the agenda, the more comfortable the adversary organization will be in allowing

you into the inner sanctum. Your competence will be appreci-
ated and *embraced*.

Let's try again with Joe.

*"Joe, I'm not sure this information has any value to you, and if
it doesn't just say so and we'll go no further. Fair? Okay. Then that's
our agreement. If it doesn't apply we'll go no further. If it does apply,
we'll move forward, okay?"*

With this agenda in place Bill isn't going to feel blindsided or
pushed to close. You've given him every right to say "no."
You've reiterated your point three times (3+). Your own emotions are under control. That's some agenda!

Before making his opening statement in the conference call in
the Network, Inc., negotiation we've been following, the president of Network said, "If you have any questions, please direct
them to me. I will be the only one responding to any questions,
unless I defer them to someone else. Is that okay with everyone?" He was negotiating what I call a mini-agenda. You may
have a major agenda and several mini-agendas, some of which
you resort to only if a problem comes up outside the scope of
the major agenda. A mini-agenda can be almost *anything,* and it
must be *everything* it needs to be. No detail is too minor.

*"May I ask you a difficult question without your getting mad at
me? You're sure I can ask you a tough question? You won't get mad?"*

That's another mini-agenda (and another 3+). With that
mini-agenda in place, you can ask the question without fear, but
asking that question out of the blue might have been enough to
send your adversary packing. Agendas and mini-agendas not
only make you comfortable, they make your *adversary* comfort-

able. By keeping your adversary comfortable, *you* maintain control and leverage.

What the Agenda Can Contain

A valid agenda or mini-agenda has five basic categories:

1. Problems
2. Our baggage
3. Their baggage
4. What we want
5. What happens next

Any given agenda can include issues in some or all of the categories, but every issue you need to negotiate—every single one—will fit into one of these five categories. Let's consider each in detail.

Problems

What are "problems"? We all know the answer, in the general sense, and I'm talking in the general sense here. A problem is anything you see as a problem. Anything! They can even be imagined, not real. How can an imagined problem be valid? If it's imagined by either party, it's in the air, and if it's in the air it has to be dealt with. So if your adversary feels she has a problem even though you don't think it's a problem, you must see it as one.

Can I be specific? Sure. Your company used to have a reputation for poor service. That issue has been solved, as any of your *current* customers know. But this negotiation is with an adversary who remembers the bad old days, who wrote you off (perhaps justifiably), and has just now been enticed to take another look. That negative memory is *definitely* a problem. Put it on the agenda—the very first agenda. Or your big company used to have the reputation with suppliers of being such a mean and nasty negotiator that topflight suppliers were driven away. They'd been burned once too often. Now you've had to change (a fanciful scenario, I admit), but many of these suppliers don't know that. You have to put your reputation on an agenda.

Let's say you sell the most expensive automobile in the world. Now, you don't make assumptions—you never make assumptions, because you never know—but you do understand that money can be a real problem for many people who would love to own this car, and you do lay this question on the table for up-front consideration. It may be the first item on your agenda for the first negotiation.

> *"Bill, I'm in the business of putting people in the finest motorcar in the world. Before we go any further, are you able to spend or finance $200,000 to buy a Rolls-Royce? It's a lot of money, we all know that. . . . Interesting. You could write a check for $200,000 if you choose to do so today? That's great. What bank would you draw the check on? . . . Oh, I see, you'd* borrow *the money from the bank before you write the check. . . . Oh, you'd borrow the money from any bank that will loan it to you? Interesting."*

You've nurtured, you've reversed, you've connected, and you've found out where things stand. Good work. Of course, this scenario is extreme, but extremes provide us with clear pictures.

Problems can be of a general nature—your company's history of poor service, the question of money—or they can be specific.

Recall the negotiation with Craig, the commercial real estate agent who needed the additional $50,000 to close the deal. The minute this became a problem it went on an agenda. If he had hidden this problem he more than likely would have lost the deal.

Here's a small sample of problems on agendas I've coached:

- We don't understand Mr. Smith's vision of his business.

- A thick glass wall exists between the two companies. We see each other but remain at a distance. This may be preventing us from gaining access to their best technology and preventing them from gaining access to our best technology.

- Our company doesn't know where the adversary is going with its new program, and therefore our preparation is impaired.

- Our company doesn't know what Company X truly requires. It would be reckless for our company to respond to their request for proposal at this time.

- Mr. Jones wouldn't come to the demonstration.

- Our company is focused on working on real opportunities with customers who see value in our technology. We don't generally put on demonstrations for every customer who requests one.

- We're getting conflicting directions from different departments of their company.

- The building we want to buy is improperly zoned.

- The building we want to sell is improperly zoned.

- We'll probably need the seller to help with financing, maybe carry a second mortgage.

- Your product is terrific, but it has always been too expensive for us. We have this negative attitude going in.

- Your company has the reputation of picking only the "low-hanging fruit," and we are a premium service.

Obviously, any list of potential problems is literally infinite. Every negotiation is different, every negotiation will have a different set of problems that crop up, but you will find that many problems relate to the major categories of my system: Who are their decision makers? What's their pain? What's their budget? In the Network, Inc., case, the new team brought in to take over for the incompetent old team had to start almost from scratch with all of the problems in that negotiation. They had to do a lot of blank slating and ask a lot of questions.

All too often, we negotiators try *not* to recognize our problems, or if we do recognize them, we're then tempted to sweep them under the carpet and hope they go away. If the problems seem insurmountable, we give up. In short, *we* are often the real problem underlying all of our problems, because we do not deal with them head-on. But if we do deal with our problems head-on, we appear as effective people to the adversary. This is comforting for the adversary and for us.

Baggage—Ours and Theirs

Baggage is our collected life experiences and observations— some old, some new, some wise, some foolish—that we carry around all the time. We may have worked our way through a lot of personal baggage, but other kinds can pop up in any negotiation. How many people do you think are burdened by baggage related to gender, age, religion, education, appearance, attitudes, financial status, experience, or seniority? Whatever baggage you think will be a problem in the negotiation needs to be dealt with up front. Some new clients are surprised to learn that such issues properly belong on the agenda. They think of an agenda as dealing only with the big issues of the final deal per se: unit price, delivery dates, and the like. "Problems" they can see, after thinking about it, but "baggage"?

My answer: Agendas and mini-agendas lay out *everything* that will significantly affect reaching that deal. Baggage is certainly in that category.

By bringing up baggage, aren't we making *assumptions,* and aren't we supposed to avoid assumptions? Shrewd questions. Baggage is the one and only area in which you can make an assumption regarding your adversary, based on your experience with other adversaries and how they've perceived you. You have to have a personal history with the issue; baggage is an *educated* guess. But if you do have any such assumptions, you should bring them up. This may be difficult for you to do, but you should be more afraid of the baggage that is neither recognized nor negotiated in the beginning.

Your adversary will *not* resent your question about baggage. He wasn't born yesterday. He'll know where you're coming from. He'll respect you for asking. Or maybe the baggage you lay on the table *does* kill the deal then and there. Maybe your adversary just won't take seriously anyone who's relatively inexperienced. (It happens.) So what's the loss if you lay your inexperience on the table and the adversary walks away? You weren't going to get anywhere anyway. You've kept your time-and-energy budget extremely low. But if your adversary does not walk off, you have gained some respect for your forthrightness and competence, and you have negotiated a track on which to run without being blindsided.

> *"George, I'm new in this business. If my inexperience is going to be a problem in this deal, let's talk about it now."*
>
> *"Yes, now's a good time. John, the only problem I have with your being new is that if we come up against something you can't handle with confidence, I want your assurance that you'll call in someone to help. Someone who really knows how to handle that problem. If that's okay with you, I'm comfortable."*
>
> *"That's fine with me. Are you sure it's okay with you?"*
>
> *"Yes, John. It's okay with me."*
>
> *"All right, that will be our deal. If I can't handle something with complete confidence, I'll call my boss to help. That's our deal. Agreed?"*
>
> *"Agreed."* [Note the 3+, of course. George agreed three times. Sometimes an agenda item simply clears the air.]
>
> *"Folks, I'm a lawyer. This a problem?"* [Laughter ensues, which represents progress, but you push ahead with 3+.] *"Seriously. We lawyers don't rank too high in the polls these days. You sure it's not a problem?"* [Everyone shakes his or her head in the negative, so you make the point for the third time.] *"No? Great. Everyone loves the fact that I'm a lawyer!"* [More laughter.]

Now you're a swell fellow and there's no need to kill all the lawyers after all. But if you hadn't brought up the question you might expect to hear, days or weeks down the line, something like this:

"Well, Bill, since this contract is so important, I'll get back to you after I've looked this over and talked with some people."

Your adversary's unstated feeling might be:

"I wouldn't trust a lawyer with the time of day. I think I'll check with the competition. I'll check with my lawyer."

Or in a different situation your adversary might reply, "I like what you've shown me, Betty. Call me back in a few weeks and I'll let you know my decision." His unstated feeling: "Widgets are a man's business. What can you know about them?" If Betty has run into such biases in the past, she must get the question out in the open immediately by saying, "John, I'm one of the few women in the widget industry. I know of one other. We're rare in this field, let's face it. Frankly, I've encountered resentment from some guys for this reason alone, that I'm a woman. What problems do you see here?" And then proceed with the 3+, no matter what John's answer is. Perhaps he won't be honest, but the fact that the question is now on the table might give him second thoughts about letting any bias affect his decisions.

More baggage I've seen in my day:

- Your chief negotiator used to work for us and had a distinctly negative experience.

- Our chief negotiator used to work for you and had a distinctly negative experience.

- Our main competitor has been your supplier for twelve years.

- We've been remiss in not calling on you for three years.

- Your manufacturing is biased against us and doesn't want to expand our role within your company.

- We have been consistently late in delivery of systems.

- You just don't believe we can do any better than our competitors.

- You believe our company is too expensive.

- You believe our company is too small for you to depend on.

- You don't like our dual pricing policy and are concerned about overseas support.

- We come dangerously close to *needing* some orders booked in the short term.

The line between problems and baggage is a thin one, obviously, and not a critical one. Baggage discarded by all concerned is not a problem. Baggage that isn't discarded remains a problem. Just be sure that *every* problem and *every* piece of baggage is placed on an agenda. Use your imagination, use your experience, use your common sense. When in doubt, err on the side of including a candidate problem or baggage on the agenda.

Wants

In addition to problems and baggage, we have "wants" as legitimate issues for an agenda. Wants can be much more complicated than either of the other categories. Consider this quick exchange.

"John, I have an idea for your business that could increase its value dramatically."

"Good, Bill. Let's see it."
"Great, John. I'll lay it out right here on the desk."

Ten minutes later:

"I like what I see, Bill. Let me study it for a week or two, then get back to me."
"Sure, John. I'll talk to you in a few weeks."

Far-fetched, you say? Stand in my shoes as a coach for a few days. I see this often in new clients. What did Bill *want* in this negotiation? From that conversation, we don't know exactly. What was the outcome? Unfortunately, this we do know: Poor Bill has spilled his beans and is now completely at the mercy of his adversary. In fact, I know of a similar situation in which the noncommittal adversary took the new idea to a third party and slipped himself into the deal as broker of record. Insult and injury!

Of all the issues in the negotiation that *should* be placed on an agenda but often are not, wants are supreme. In this regard, they are our greatest cause of failure. Often negotiators don't know what they want—not really—not step by step by step by step down the long and winding road. They just want a signed deal, that's all. They don't have a clue about what they want at every step of the decision-making process *along the way*. They're thinking about ends, which are out of their control, not about means, which we control with agendas.

Without a clear understanding and picture of what we want at every point in the negotiation, we can't put it on an agenda. And if we can't put it on an agenda, we have no right to ask for it. And if we can't ask for it, we put ourselves completely at the mercy of the adversary. So if we want to stay in control to the

extent possible—and we do—what we want must be part of
every agenda. (Want, not *need*. We don't need anything, of
course.)

Granted, it's often difficult to figure out what we want, but
figuring this out will make you "rich" in agenda. You can make
all the negotiating mistakes in the world, but if you get a handle
on what you want, and get these wants placed on an agenda negotiated with the adversary, you've got a chance.

How could incompetent Bill's negotiation with John have
been structured to keep Bill in control? First, Bill has to ask himself what he wants at this earliest stage of the negotiation. What
he wants—or should want—is to protect his ideas. The following would have been a productive approach:

> *"John, if I had an idea for your business that could increase its
> value dramatically over the next five years, who would be involved in
> the decision process?"*
>
> *"Bill, I make all those decisions."*
>
> *"Of course you do, but who would give you good advice in finan-
> cial areas?"*
>
> *"Well, Bill, I'm the guy, but I would want my attorney and tax
> man to look at it."*
>
> *"I see. John, who else would you get involved?"*
>
> *"No one else, that would be the group."*
>
> *"John, here is what I'd like you to do. I have an idea drawn up.
> I'd like to show it to you. If you like it, can you and I show it to your
> attorney and accountant together? Of course, if you don't like it,
> we'll drop it. Fair?"*
>
> *"Sounds fair to me."*
>
> *"Okay John, our deal is that if you like my idea, we'll go together
> to see the attorney and the tax man. Please sign this 'broker of record'*

to protect my ideas. This says that others can't take my ideas and use them without my being paid. John, are you comfortable with protecting my work?"

"Sure, I have no problem. If you do the work, you get paid."

"Are you sure you're okay with this, John?"

"I have no problem with it, Bill. It's only fair. Let me sign it."

Bill, by asking a few questions of himself and coming up with what he wanted right then, was able to negotiate an agenda over which he could have some control. Of course, this doesn't mean he will get the deal. He still has difficult negotiations ahead. But at least he has a chance to get things off on the right foot.

Knowing what we want out of each stage of the negotiation—what we want on each agenda—helps us make sure that our mission and purpose is clear. It guarantees that our goals are clear. It makes us think clearly how to proceed—A, B, C, D, E, and all the way to Z and a deal that sticks.

But what if John won't sign the proposed agreement? Well, find out now. If we know from the beginning what we want, there is no need to compromise and no danger of being sucker punched later.

If you can't figure out what you want at a given point in the negotiation, figure out what else is missing. Is your mission and purpose in place? If you haven't prepared for the negotiation session, how aware can you be of what you want from that session? Not very. But if you know exactly what you want, how are you perceived by the adversary? Effective. If you know exactly what you want and it's valid, how early do you compromise? You don't compromise early.

Take a look at these "wants," most from assorted actual negotiations, a few generic:

- We want to share our vision of our business and how the negotiation should proceed.

- We want our company to be seen by your company as committed to your success.

- We want your feedback on our suggestion about changing the rate scale.

- We want a meeting to discuss the latest changes in your proposal.

- We want your full support of our programs.

- We want an *objective* comparison of our service vis-à-vis our competitors' service.

- We want you to understand that this field is changing rapidly, and we want you to see where your decision on pricing could be taking you in the future.

- We want a clear, complete picture from you of exactly what you need from us at this stage.

- We want an introduction with the president, the one and only decision maker in the company.

- We want a demonstration of your product.

- We want you to assure us that your inventory and production line can meet the requirements of this enhanced schedule.

- We want the termite report.

- We want your financial statement.

- We want your résumé.

- We want the first draft of the contract.

- We want more time to reply to your RFP (Request for Proposal).

- We want a definite date by which you will respond to our RFP.

The list could be infinite. For just a single complicated actual negotiation, it could be pages long. A great exercise is to sit down and think about a "typical" negotiation in your field—if there is such a thing—and draw up a list of wants along the way. The really complete list will be pretty long.

Now, I want to take a closer look at the list above, because these wants are not quite sharp enough. Think about this question: What does every want entail from the adversary? A decision, of course. This is almost by definition, because any progress depends on decisions. Therefore, I'd like you to consider each want in the negotiation in terms of the decision required of the adversary in order to fulfill it. And of course the decision may always be "no." You allow every opportunity for your adversary to say "no." And of course you are wary of any "yes" and extremely wary of any "maybe."

So we could revise that list in this way:

- We want you to reject or accept our vision of our business and how the negotiation should proceed.

- We want to know whether you do or do not see our company as committed to your success.

- We want you to reject or accept our proposed change in the rate scale.

- We want you to reject or accept a meeting to discuss the latest changes in your proposal.

- We want to know whether you do or do not fully support our programs.

- We want you to either submit or refuse to submit the termite report.

- We want you to either refuse or grant us more time to reply to your RFP.

This is a good exercise to help you understand that every want does indeed require decisions by the adversary. By framing your wants in terms of those decisions, you discipline yourself to live in the world of the adversary—a theme of my entire system, of course.

In most negotiations, at some point one of your wants will be some numbers—prices, quantities—but always remember that numbers are limitations. Avoid them until the time is right. (A very recent example: After quoting a $185 unit cost in a pre-Camp negotiation with a large customer, a client just received $290 in the Camp era. This can happen much more often than you realize.)

As the buyer, you do *not* want to know the seller's prices in the first meeting unless this is an extremely simple negotiation. As the seller, you do *not* want to know how much the customer says he wants to pay in the first meeting. Wants proceed in lock-step with the other principles of my system. Your first wants will concern the big picture: your adversary's baggage, perhaps, and certainly his vision and pain and needs and budgets.

What Happens Next

The last agenda item is "what happens next." How many times have you been in a negotiation and assumed that when the other party said "Call us back" they really meant it, but when you did call they were busy and couldn't talk? How often is a brush-off like "I'll talk to you in a few weeks" accepted by a neophyte negotiator who gets sucked into small talk, gets uncomfortable, leaves the subject, makes assumptions, doesn't conclude business? It happens all the time, because we get lost in the emotion of the final moments of a meeting or phone call. But you must learn very quickly to take care of business by carefully negotiating what happens next.

As with finding the decision maker, this may seem like an innocuous item for an agenda, but, believe me, it's not. It protects us against unwarranted assumptions (not that you have assumptions of any kind, other than baggage). It's a leg up on the next agenda. It's simply mandatory. And, of course, what happens next must be *negotiated* with the adversary, and it must be verified three times.

Enough Said

The logic is simple: By crafting agendas, you find out where you stand. By putting these agendas into action, you *improve* this standing.

13

Present Your Case—If You Insist

Beware the Seductions of PowerPoint

IN MANY FIELDS of business, and therefore in many negotiations, the presentation is the formal act of showing off the
product or service, stating features and benefits and prices, and
requesting a formal response: *This is my widget, this is what it will
do, this is why it's so much better than any other widget on the market,
this is how much it costs, how many do you want to buy right now?*
This show-and-tell often follows the RFP, and on this subject I
am probably as contrarian as I can get. To the chagrin of some of
my own clients, frankly, I say that the presentation is that part of
basic negotiating theory—win-win and otherwise—that the old
school may feel has tremendous value but in fact has very little, if
any. I've seen many more times when the presentation was positively *harmful* to the presenter's standing in the negotiation, or
even fatal. I say instead that the greatest presentation you will

ever give is the one your adversary never sees. I'd like to repeat that statement: The greatest presentation you will ever give is the one your adversary never sees.

In opening my defense of this position I pose these interrogative-led questions: When was the last time you hoped that the salesperson/agent/whoever would just be quiet for five minutes and let you discover the offer for yourself? How many times have you walked into a store and a salesperson immediately attached himself to you like a limpet? Plenty, I imagine. Most of us would rather be left alone to look around for ourselves, and then to find help and ask questions when we're ready to. Now, how many times have you listened to formal business presentations and been moved to take action on the spot? Never, I'm betting. It's a silly formality, at best, or more likely an insidious ploy to get the adversary to spill her beans to no purpose.

If you've worked through your system and implanted vision and painted your adversary's pain effectively, you have made a winning presentation.

One of my best clients was initially as skeptical of my system as anyone who has ever worked with me. I don't even understand why he decided to stay on board, because the system seemed so contrarian as to be somehow "countercultural" for him, and he is not a counterculture kind of guy. But he has come to excel in his negotiations. He's in commercial real estate, where requests for RFPs are pretty much standard—except with him. It doesn't matter if he's dealing with—negotiating with—a city zoning board or a Japanese conglomerate. If he creates a clear picture of pain, with vision to follow, he does not need to make any formal presentation. This man is a good negotiator, but he is not a magician. If the system can work for him, it can work for anyone in real estate.

A major tenet of my system is that you want the negotiation to take place—where? In the world of your adversary. To this end you ask interrogative-led questions, and your adversary's answers create vision for him or her. You don't *tell* anyone anything, remember. They have to *see* it for themselves. But how do most presentations work? They try to *tell* the adversary not just anything but *everything,* and then hope against hope that the adversary goes along with what's been said. But the presentation, by definition, puts the adversary into the intellectual mode. When the adversary is in the intellectual mode, he raises objections, doesn't he? Think about this from your own experience. When someone presents to you, your instinct is to hunt for objections, quibbles, and mistakes, and you always find them. The classic presentation serves only to create objections, so you end up *answering* questions rather than *asking* them.

When I frame the issue with presentations this way in workshops, I see a lot of bobbing heads in the audience. They know I'm onto something here.

If you have worked effectively to paint the pain, a presentation is simply a waste of time and energy. If you have *not* painted the pain, the presentation is no substitute for your failure to do so, and it won't do you any good now. What are you going to present? How do you know that the points of your presentation have any interest to the adversary? You don't, because you don't know their pain. So anyone who wants to "present" to me is telling me that they haven't painted the pain. He doesn't know what the pain is. If he did, he wouldn't be presenting blindly, throwing mud at the wall and hoping that some of it sticks.

Furthermore, a presentation shows neediness, doesn't it? Can't it often seem to the adversary to be a rush to close? Can't it come across as taking away the right to say "no"? Indeed it can and does. Or you want to present because this negotiation is going nowhere, and the presentation is your last hope. Or maybe the adversary has insisted upon the presentation, as a ploy. So you do your thing and lay out all your beans and show 'em how great you are and accomplish what, really? Don't take my word for it. Think honestly about your own experience and I'll bet you agree that otherwise effective negotiations have *survived* formal presentations, but they have never needed them.

> *"We need a presentation on your business."*
>
> *"Well, I don't have any idea how to do that. I really don't. If I had an idea where you stand, what you need, what you're interested in, then I'd be happy to address your concerns. That's what I'm here for. What's driving you to ask me for a presentation? I mean, why do you want my widget? You've been dealing with USA Widgets for seven years. You must have the best price in the world from them by now. How could we ever compete with USA Widgets? Why are you now interested in Widgets International?"*
>
> *"But you called us."*
>
> *"Yes, and I'm glad I did. I was interested in how it's going with USA Widgets. There must be some reason why you invited me to this meeting. You must have some interest in something about Widgets International. I just need an idea what it is."*

That's not an entirely fanciful exchange. That's an effective way to deal with RFPs, an effective way to get the ball rolling, even if you have to do a little something official looking toward the end of the negotiation.

One client once struck a deal worth a couple of hundred million dollars with a multinational by getting the *adversary* to make the presentation. After ten or so months of serious work by my client in finding the decision makers—always a challenge with a multinational—painting the pain, and building budgets, the adversary finally asked us for our presentation of how much of our product they should buy at what unit cost, and so on. We suggested that it made a lot more sense for them to give us their thoughts and give us a good idea where they were going and what they were trying to do, and *then* we could respond with ideas tailored to their requirements. That's a good idea, they said.

If You Insist

If, for whatever reason I *oppose,* you make a formal presentation, at least do it well. First, be certain that you are presenting to the real decision makers. If you make a formal presentation to the unqualified, you're spilling your beans all over the universe. Second, you must have an agenda negotiated in advance of the big day. The adversary must know, *Here we go, the formal presentation.* The adversary must know what the presentation will contain, and what it will not contain. The adversary must know that it is finally "yes" or "no" time. "Maybe" is not allowed as an answer following the presentation. Make sure this agreement is negotiated on an agenda. If it's not, what will you do when you hear the dreaded "maybe"? Finally—and I hope by this point in the book this statement almost goes without saying—always present in the world of the adversary. Granted, you're telling them things rather than letting them see, by the nature of the presentation, but at least tell them things about the issues that are driving the negotiation. Present *only* the information that addresses your adversary's concern, the information that addresses the adversary's pain—or what you know about it, which is probably not much, or you wouldn't be presenting in the first place.

Resist the temptation to throw in the kitchen sink. If the only pain is the tire's maximum carrying capacity, forget about how wide your tires are. If you're trying to sell a house that has a beautiful lawn but the buyer hasn't expressed any interest in a beautiful lawn, stifle the temptation to deliver a long spiel on the subject. Let the grass speak for itself. You can always bring it up later, if the occasion arises. ("Addition by subtraction": this old sports adage about making your team better by getting rid of a certain player is also true for presentations.) Present in the order of importance: "Mr. Smith, since your most important concern is horsepower, let's look at the engine first. Then we'll check out the headroom for the driver's seat, since you're rather tall and I know that's also important to you."

Now recall from chapter 3 the football recruit who used my system. He never made the formal presentation of an application to the school he finally chose—and that chose him—but he did provide a demonstration—a videotape—and the key point about his demonstration pertains to presentations. Most recruits make the mistake of submitting film that is in their own world: clips of their spectacular runs, spectacular catches, touchdowns. But is this what the coach really wants to see? If it's not, if the coach's pain is elsewhere, the recruit has not presented to that pain. The way to find out is to ask the question this recruit asked of every coach: "How do you evaluate a player?" Isn't this question just common sense? Yes. But is it commonly asked? No. Our recruit found out that the answer varied from coach to coach and often seemed very limited. One coach was mainly interested in vertical jumping ability, another in speed, another in strength work (specifically, the bench press). One coach would not recruit a defensive back under six feet tall, and another would not recruit any players under six feet tall. In any event, no coach said or implied, *Send me clips of your greatest plays.* So our recruit tailored his videotape to the answers provided by each coach. He presented in the world of each specific coach, not his own world. He showed them what he had decided *they* wanted to see, not what he thought they should want to see, or what he wanted to see of himself. That approach took a lot of discipline and a lot of work.

In short, if you insist on making formal presentations, or if a hidebound or stealthy adversary insists that you make one, do it well. Stay within the system. It's perfectly okay to pull out all the stops with overheads, art, graphics, multimedia, and everything else that PowerPoint and the other software programs offer, but none of this works if you're relying on the glitz by itself to carry the day. It won't. If your high-tech presentation isn't addressed to your adversary's vision and pain, you're wasting your giga-bytes. (And if you've negotiated well up to this point, you've wasted them anyway.)

The Next Negotiation

What is prep-end step? It's the reminder that your work in *this* negotiating session isn't over until you've either prepared the bridge to the next one by means of "what happens next" on the agenda, or until you have prepared a means of exiting the nego-tiation for good—ending it by fading away into the night. Prep-end step works hand in hand with "what happens next" to ensure that the negotiation is organized and to the point. In the Network, Inc., negotiation we've looked at several times, the president outlined the problem and told the adversary what he wanted—for the other company to propose a solution—and then he said, "And when you have offered a solution, we will be happy to sit with you face-to-face. With twenty-four-hours' notice, my team will meet you anywhere in the world. Just call me back and tell me where."

That's prep-end step. That's advising the adversary of the bridge to the next negotiation. Two days after the conference call, the adversary requested an immediate meeting in Germany. As we know, good things happened in the end.

Now I switch to the negotiation I introduced in chapter 3 between the company I call Bonanza, Inc., and the big multinational, the one in which Bonanza got tired of being whipsawed in competition with two other companies for a big project. Bonanza had about fifteen men and women working on this deal with their various counterparts with the multinational. I'd say that all in all, we had about five hundred negotiating sessions of one sort or another, including e-mailed mini-negotiations. This was just a really complicated situation. Plotted on paper, all the negotiations within the negotiation would look like a tangled spider's web. In fact, however, all these bits and pieces of the negotiation fit together logically, thanks to agendas and diligent prep-end stepping every step of the way. Not a single e-mail or phone call was concluded without setting the stage for the next e-mail or phone call. The end result was that Bonanza now has a special relationship with the multinational. (With many multinationals, such alliances are often meaningless, or even dangerous. This one isn't.)

Not only is your work not over after this negotiating session, it's not over after this entire negotiation is signed, sealed, and delivered. The signed contract is just another decision. Isn't this right? Contracts are broken all the time, for starters. More important, most contracts entail future obligations from both parties, almost by definition. Agreements have been made *to do something.* Some good or service has to be delivered, exchanged, or bartered by one party or another, or by both. Something has to work right. Something is guaranteed. So drink the champagne, by all means, but don't then drop your guard. Be ready for more negotiations. As history has demonstrated all too often over the past millennia, keeping the peace is much more important and usually much more difficult than signing the peace treaty. That's what prep-end step is all about.

Prep-end step is also about how to end the negotiation short of agreement. It happens in straight sales, it happens in proposed multibillion-dollar corporate mergers. You have a budget for the negotiation, you have your mission and purpose, and this deal just isn't going to happen. This finally becomes clear. You decide the time has come to retire. When this happens, I recommend the calm, quiet "Thanks but no thanks, maybe next time." To my mind, this fadeaway is far more effective than burning bridges. I hate to see clients burn their bridges, no matter how ill-served they feel. For one thing, it betrays neediness on their part. They wouldn't feel the temptation to burn bridges if they didn't have too much invested emotionally. For another, who knows what will happen in the future? Complete changes of heart or mind are not unknown, after all. I just can't see any advantage to burned bridges except some kind of short-term self-validation, and that kind of neediness is not good enough, not in my system.

One final story about the value of prep-end step, a fairly long but instructive one. One of my early students, Eric, was a college dropout working, like his father, in the life insurance business—a real crucible for negotiation skills. One of Eric's first sales calls was with an elderly lady living in a retirement center. He found the lady's pain—she had one-third of a million dollars sitting in the bank—helped her see this pain—she could do a whole lot better—had a budget, understood her decision-making process, and established an agenda with which he would try to help the lady fix her pain. When Eric's sales manager found out the size of the negotiation, he became excited, sales manager fashion, and insisted that he go along to help Eric *close* the deal. Eric immediately negotiated a separate deal with the sales manager: He could come along, but only if he kept his mouth shut. He knew nothing about Eric's system of negotiation. He could blow it.

The negotiation opened as planned and went extremely well with our nineteen-year-old negotiator and his sixty-seven-year-old adversary. She decided to give Eric three checks for $100,000 each. At this point, Eric did exactly what prep-end step, "Never Close," the 3+ technique, and nurturing call for: He slid the three checks back across the table to his prospective client and asked her, "Are you sure this is what you want to do? I don't want you to do this unless you are sure this is something you want to do." He gave the client every opportunity in the world to say no. Almost predictably, the conventional sales manager started to interrupt, but Eric kicked him under the table.

Now I'll let Eric pick up the story as he related it later to me:

"Jim, I was comfortable, but I thought my sales manager was going to have a heart attack. He had no concept of what I was doing. He didn't see that I was preparing for the next negotiation. Of course I wanted to help my client, but I also wanted to get my referral system in high gear, and if this wasn't handled properly, I would receive no referrals from this lady. As the meeting closed, I spoke privately with her. She whispered that when I came back with the other documents I needed to deliver, I shouldn't bring the other 'fellow' with me.

She didn't know why, but she didn't trust him. Two days later, she called to tell me she had been talking with her friends at the retirement community, and they would like to invite me over to discuss how I might help them like I helped her. Jim, I am convinced prepend step was the key to gaining eleven new clients."

I am convinced Eric was right.

14

Life's Greatest Lesson
The Only Assurance
of Long-Term Success

IN ANY ROLE in life, including negotiation, there is a direct correlation between our self-image and our performance. We consistently perform to the level of our self-image. Our world was built by men and women of high self-esteem. In negotiation, it is absolutely required if you are to succeed. It is self-esteem that gives you the confidence to face down debilitating neediness, to swallow false pride, to make tough decisions, to act in the many challenging ways I've discussed throughout these pages. This last chapter in my book is as important as any of them.

Is it clear that there's no contradiction between having high self-esteem and allowing your *adversary* to be okay? Self-esteem is your internal appraisal of yourself as an individual, and nothing can affect it. Okayness is your *public* presentation of yourself.

The difference is huge, obviously. Your own high self-esteem is exactly what allows you to allow your adversary to have all the okayness in the negotiation.

Self-esteem keeps you in the fight when you face overwhelming odds. With it, no situation can keep you from seeing yourself as a strong person, a capable person, a deserving person, a successful person. High self-image gives us the strength to endure high levels of success. It confirms your desire to fulfill your capabilities. It demands that you be paid full measure for work rendered. It is your high self-image that won't allow you to sleep if you don't do the right thing.

On the other hand, those of us with low self-image will not pay the price of victory. We will quit. Bill Gates did not take on the federal government while burdened with low self-esteem. In fact, I challenge anyone to find examples of greatness in any field produced by individuals with low self-esteem.

Think of the child who is called clumsy by the critical parent, told he has "two left feet." What success would you expect of this child in the roll of athlete? Not much. How many children have you known who wouldn't even try an activity out of fear of embarrassment? How many children are called "dumb" at a young age? How many embrace "dumb" as a *self-image* and prove it true? How many times have you heard someone say, "I just can't see myself doing that"? But what if they say, "I'm going to do everything I can to do that"? Which person has the self-image that will give him or her a chance to make their dream come true?

But I am not a fatalist. I do not believe our destinies are set in stone by age three or even thirty. Certainly, early successes and failures play a role in the development of self-esteem, but anyone—*anyone*—can achieve, maintain, and deserve a much *higher* self-image if he or she is committed to the task. And this observation brings me to the main point of this chapter, paying forward, which I introduce with a final story about coach Woody Hayes.

In 1975, Ohio State played a great Michigan team coached by Bo Schembechler. It was a typical Woody versus Bo matchup, both teams undefeated and rated among the top three teams in the nation. This was a championship prizefight with two tough heavyweights trying to knock each other out. Through the first three and a half quarters, it was a close game. Then, late in the fourth quarter, Ohio State All-American Ray Griffin intercepted a Michigan pass and returned it to the three yard line. What a knockout blow! Buckeye fans went nuts, of course, not only in Ann Arbor, where the game was played, but around the world. Once again Ohio State was on the way to the Rose Bowl.

When the team returned to Columbus from Ann Arbor, it was met at the airport by some twenty thousand fans. To signify the victory and the upcoming appearance in Pasadena, a group of these fans gave a dozen red roses to each of the women who had traveled with the team in any capacity. Then Coach Hayes did a strange thing. He immediately confiscated all the roses and put them in his El Camino truck. No one understood what he was doing, nor was he telling. In fact, he never did say what he did with the flowers. Only later did I learn that he had driven, with only five hours of sleep the night before, from hospital to hospital in Columbus, presenting a rose to every terminally ill patient he could find, until the flowers ran out.

Coach Hayes was putting into practice the lesson learned explicitly from Emerson and taught implicitly by the great religions of the world, the lesson he had taught his players at Ohio State and everyone else he dealt with all over the country: In this world, you must "pay forward" because you can't really pay others back, not sufficiently. With those roses distributed in the hospital on the day after the great victory, Coach Hayes was paying forward. (*Pay It Forward* was the title of a film in 2000, which combined this idea with that of a chain letter.)

Do you remember the feelings you had as a child when you received presents? You were thrilled. But, as thrilled as you might have been to receive, do you remember when you went out and earned your very own money and took those hard-earned dollars and bought someone you loved a present? How good did it feel when that person became excited? I once gave my devoted grandmother an oil painting of a seascape. She was so overwhelmed, she cried. It was the most thrilling day of my life. Why do the wealthy give their money away? They can't take it with them, it's true, and they want to avoid taxes, and many don't want to bestow *too much* on their children (smart thinking), but they also do it to feel better about themselves. The very wealthy can have self-image problems like everyone else.

Philanthropy is paying forward. Tithing to a house of worship is paying forward. So is patriotic sacrifice. So is sleeping in hospitals with the wounded, as President Lincoln did. Queen Isabella I of Spain was paying forward when she wrote a check to Columbus to go explore the unknown, over five hundred years ago. An old man in Iowa, the owner of a large grain elevator, was paying forward when he told a young man working in a gas station that he would pay for his college tuition if he promised to work hard. This was during the Great Depression. Without this assistance, the young man would have stayed at that gas station, in all likelihood. With this aid, Roy M. Kottman went to Iowa State, eventually became dean of agriculture at the Ohio State

University, and played a major role in the development of hybrid corns that increased yields fourfold and helped to feed the world.

There's nothing new in these paragraphs. The context may be unusual, but I am speaking of age-old wisdom. Achievement requires self-esteem, and to build self-esteem you only need to start paying forward, to pay forward more effectively, at every opportunity, with your family and friends, in the workplace, in your community, in your house of worship, everywhere. And then you should pay forward some more. You will reap the benefit in every aspect of your life, including most definitely the negotiating table.

Throughout this book I've discussed attitudes and behaviors and activities vital for negotiation success. Paying forward is as important as any of them. It is the most dramatic way to see yourself as a good person, a successful person, a contributor to society. It is the most dramatic way to *be* this individual. Paying forward is the secret for creating self-esteem, no matter what your age or circumstances. *Anyone* can pay forward. There are absolutely no excuses on this one.

You can even pay forward in the bare-knuckles world of business. In illustration, I want to tell one final story. This story goes back to the mid-1950s, when the queen of England decided to put up for sale the land she owned in the Lake Muskoka region of Ontario, Canada. This land had never been owned by any white man before the queen. It had been taken from the original Canadians by treaty. My dad bid for a lot, sight unseen, on Go Home Lake, and to his family's delight, his bid was accepted. In our first visit to our new holding, my father met an old trapper and hunter on the lake named Joe Bolier. Joe was starting to build summer cabins for new people on the lake—people like us. He had a small crew of workmen from the local area, and he was opening a small trading post. Dad and Joe negotiated for our new cabin, and a deal was struck with a handshake. Nothing was put in writing. The cabin would be ready when we returned next summer.

Right on schedule, we showed up with enough old furniture and other stuff to make the new cottage our summer home. Joe stopped by to say hello and to be sure Dad was happy with his work. Dad was happy, and he said so. Then he looked Joe in the eye and asked if *he* was happy with the deal. Joe said, "Well, Larry, I didn't do well here. I lost money. I underestimated the cost to carry all the lumber up over the cliffs." Dad didn't blink an eye and asked, "Joe, would another $800 cover your loss and give you a fair profit?"

The man was startled. He hadn't met many landowners like my father, but this was the right thing to do on Dad's part, and as a businessman he knew it was. Honestly, I think Dad, as an American, was a little uncomfortable in Canada. He wanted to feel good about his presence in the country. He was protecting his high self-image by doing the right thing. He was paying line for line, deed for deed. Dad was paying forward for a lifetime of service from Joe. We didn't have to worry about snow on the roof, that's for sure. Joe stayed in business on Go Home Lake and helped many other people with the small profit he earned from my father.

My father did not need the self-satisfaction of getting every last dollar out of every last negotiation. He wanted fair value. If he knew he was getting such value, he was happy to pay full price. I'm the same way. Paying full price, when justified, empowers me to *ask* full price, when justified. In this world we do usually get what we pay for, remember. We also perform to the level of our self-image.

Conclusion

Dance with the Tiger!
Thirty-three Rules to Remember

WE'RE ALL PROFESSIONAL negotiators, aren't we? Most of us don't think of ourselves this way, but we're all trying to make agreements every day. We're *negotiating*. Some of us do so haphazardly, maybe even lackadaisically, while some of us realize that since we're always negotiating, the more skillfully we do so, the better off we'll be. Presumably the readers of this book are in this latter category; you want to be better negotiators. You understand that there are levels of qualification, just as there are with any skill. The purpose of this book has been to provide you with the most basic, minimal qualification in a system that can profoundly change your life in negotiation. Now you take it from here.

I wrote in the introduction that my system is pretty easy to understand in its basics but requires discipline and patience and practice. I'll stand by that statement here in the conclusion, but I do realize that learning doesn't come automatically—not at all—and that many readers will have difficulty implementing some of the more counterintuitive principles of my system—"just say no," for example. I know this about the readers because I know it about my clients. New ones always require a considerable adjustment period. Many have been negotiating cream puffs their entire business lives—always worried whether they're being sufficiently win-win-ish—and now I'm asking them to go out and tell someone "no"!

The adjustment takes time. As I've said, eight hundred hours, according to one study I give credence to.

So how, exactly, should you go about settling in with the Camp System? First, and as I've suggested from time to time in the book, I recommend you try out the most straightforward, discrete principles and rules of the system. At the end of this conclusion I'll list thirty-three succinct rules—a nice, catchy number—that serve well as a summary of the system, as catalysts, as jogs to the memory. The rules are not listed in any particular order, because everything within my system connects with everything else, so every rule works in conjunction with every other rule. Before you read this book, most of them, such as "No Closing," would have made no sense whatsoever. By this point they definitely should make at least some sense. When you read "No Closing," you know I'm talking about neediness on your own part, which you want to control, and about anxiety on your adversary's part about feeling pressured, which you want to avoid. Likewise, you know that "No Talking" also refers to neediness on your own part, to the necessity to blank slate, and also as a reminder that asking questions and listening is preferable to answering questions and talking. "The clearer the picture of pain, the easier the decision-making process" reminds us that we cannot tell anyone anything, but can only help them *see for themselves* the pain that has brought them to the table.

Every day or week, perhaps, jot down as many of these rules as you feel comfortable handling, review them in the morning, then try them out during the day, off and on, here and there. Find a fairly risk-free situation in which you can say "no," and be sure to toss in some nurturing and an interrogative-led question as well: "Amanda, I can't do that. I just can't, but I sure want to work with you. How can we find an alternative solution?"

In a situation in which you feel a little conflict brewing, simply ask, "What would you like me to do, Jonathan? I'm at your service."

Try the Columbo effect in an innocuous situation and be a little unokay: run out of ink, run out of battery power, whatever.

When you find yourself talking too much, try the simplest reverse there is, combined with an interrogative-led question: "But enough from me, Pete. How do you see all this falling into place?"

The following day or the following week, jot down a different set of rules, and the following week, yet another set. Mix them up, because they all work together. At this "test-drive" stage, you're not trying to put these activities in a broad context, necessarily. All you're trying to do is convince yourself that they work. Two goals will be achieved: You'll become comfortable with them, and you'll see that they *do* work. You'll have a lot more hits than misses.

Why? You will be implementing valid *goals*—behavior and activity over which you can exercise control. Watching out for neediness, asking good questions, being unokay, saying and requesting "no," blank slating: These are all valid behavioral goals. In chapter 5, I mentioned the daily track that my clients maintain as a way to monitor their behavior and emotions as they affect the negotiating process. That critical assessment of behavioral goals helps us pinpoint our weaknesses, work with our strengths, and develop self-esteem. It helps us assess how we're spending our time, how we're absorbing the material, how we're doing as a negotiator. I urge you to set up your own daily track, a sheet on which you ask yourself how often and how well you have controlled your neediness, been unokay, said "no" and asked for "no," nurtured, reversed, used the 3+ technique, connected, asked interrogative-led questions, taken great notes, accepted a bad decision and corrected it with your next one, and contained your emotions. I realize it's easy for me to make this request, and it's even easy for you to plan to do something like this, but in today's hectic world it's difficult to actually do so. I'm under no illusions here, and as a coach in absentia I don't enjoy any powers of oversight, much less enforcement, but the exercise will pay dividends for everyone who gives it a try.

Now You're Ready to Give the Camp System a Simple Try

So, in the first stage you get comfortable with basic principles, basic goals, basic behaviors and activities. And you are always paying forward, of course, building self-esteem. How long do you devote to this stage? I have no idea. However long it takes for you to become comfortable enough to proceed to the second stage. You move from the test drive to the shakedown cruise, if I can mix the metaphor. You're ready to implement the system in one specific negotiation. I'd choose a pretty straightforward one, a situation that you feel comfortable with already, maybe not the most important one in the shop right now. I'd say to myself, "Okay, here we go with the Camp System. Let's just see what happens."

You're not expecting a mistake-free performance; your neediness is under control. I suggest beginning this first test negotiation with a five-step process.

First, you make certain you have a good, strong mission and purpose that's set in the world of your adversary, one that is designed to let the adversary see and decide that the benefits and features of your product or service or whatever are what they wish to acquire. (See chapter 4.)

Second, you make sure that you know the adversary's real pain—the real reason they're negotiating. You ask questions, you create vision. (See chapter 9.)

Third, you assess all the budgets involved—time-and-energy, money, and emotional investment—for both you and your adversary. You never forget about these budgets, you monitor them at all times, and you see how they seem to be influencing the decisions on both sides. (See chapter 10.)

Fourth, you make certain you're dealing with the real decision makers. (See chapter 11.)

Fifth, you don't make a phone call, you don't write an e-mail, without writing down an agenda for that phone call or e-mail. (See chapter 12.)

Of course, I label these activities "first" through "fifth," but you might be dealing with one or more at the same time. And as you're setting up the basic path for the negotiation, you're always reminding yourself about the behavior goals you practiced in stage one. You blank slate, ask the good questions, and so on. It's all part of the same package.

Periodically, you sit back and take stock, not just with a daily track of your behavior goals, but of this negotiation specifically. You take it slow and easy. You expect to feel uncomfortable when saying no. You may be so used to "taking meetings" during a negotiation that you struggle to figure out exactly what the agenda is for this meeting. But you also come to appreciate that yes, by focusing on things you can control at every stage, such as agenda, the negotiation does move forward—maybe quickly, maybe slowly, but forward. Or maybe it doesn't. Maybe it's going nowhere. If so, you have the tools to figure out why. Is your M&P valid after all? Do you really understand your adversary's pain? Do *they*?

Slowly you acquire a sense of how the pieces of the puzzle can come together. That negotiation wraps up, one way or the other. You think about how things went, then you pick another negotiation to do Camp-style, and you start again. First you crawl, then you walk, and then . . . you *dance*. This is when it really gets fun.

How long before you feel completely comfortable on the dance floor? Without training, I don't think you'll ever feel *completely* comfortable. The study and practice of negotiation is extraordinarily complicated, as you know. Every negotiation is different, and every human being is a handful, so to speak. Full and complete implementation of the system in this book requires a great deal of discipline, as I've stated time and again, and it's difficult to maintain such discipline in any endeavor when working alone. This is one reason why almost no top athletes train alone.

So how long before you're *relatively* comfortable? That may also be asking too much without training. How long before you feel *a lot more comfortable* than you may feel right now? You could reach that level within a couple of months—if you're a genius at this. It could be six months, it could be longer. It depends on how hard you work and your native talent. All I know is this: Every day you'll become more adept with the system and more confident that it works and more knowledgeable about how and why it works. Every day you'll be a better negotiator than you were yesterday, and one day, *for the first time in your business life,* you'll start to achieve at a level approaching your potential.

I guarantee it.

The Thirty-three Rules

- Every negotiation is an agreement between two or more parties with all parties having the right to veto—the right to say "no."

- Your job is not to be liked. It is to be respected and effective.

- Results are *not* valid goals.

- Money has nothing to do with a valid mission and purpose.

- Never, ever, spill your beans in the lobby—or anywhere else.

- Never enter a negotiation—never make a phone call—without a valid agenda.

- The only valid goals are those you can control: behavior and activity.

- Mission and purpose must be set in the *adversary's* world; our world must be secondary.

- Spend maximum time on payside activity and minimum time on nonpayside activity.

- You do *not* need it. You only *want* it.

- No saving. You cannot save the adversary.

- Only one person in a negotiation can feel okay. That person is the adversary.

- All action—all decision—begins with vision. Without vision, there is no action.

- Always show respect to the blocker.

- All agreements must be clarified point by point and sealed three times (using 3+).

- The clearer the picture of pain, the easier the decision-making process.

- The value of the negotiation increases by multiples as time, energy, money, and emotion are spent.

- No talking.

- Let the adversary save face at all times.

- The greatest presentation you will ever give is the one your adversary will never see.

- A negotiation is only over when we want it to be over.

- "No" is good, "yes" is bad, "maybe" is worse.

- Absolutely no closing.

- Dance with the tiger.

- Our greatest strength is our greatest weakness (Emerson).

- Paint the pain.

- Mission and purpose drive everything.

- Decisions are 100 percent emotional.

- Interrogative-led questions drive vision.

- Nurture.

- No assumptions. No expectations. Only blank slate.

- Who are the decision makers? Do you know *all* of them?

- Pay forward.

Acknowledgments

To bring a book to the world requires more than just knowledge of, and experience with, the subject—in this case, negotiation. Without the confidence, vision, and talents of my partners, Bob Jordan and Patty and Mike Bryan, this book would not be in your hands. I also wish to thank John Thornton, especially, and Joe Spieler of the Spieler Literary Agency, who helped shape this project and place it with Crown Business, and Ruth Mills and then John Mahaney, who inherited the project and brought it to fruition with intelligence and energy.

Successful coaches must have talented players to work with. I have been extremely fortunate in this regard, and to these men and women I express my sincerest gratitude. For obvious reasons I will not name you, but your success is a joy to me every day, and your faith and trust will never be forgotten.

A successful coach also requires a foundation of principles and truths learned from great coaches, teachers, mentors, associates, and respected opponents. First among these have been my father, Lawrence R. Camp, and my grandfather Richard Barlow. I will be forever grateful for their guidance and leadership.

Coaches

Irving P. Olmstead	Woody Hayes	Dick Eaton
Duffy Daughtery	Col. L. A. Bienvenu	Fred Taylor
Maj. Dave Miller	John Mummey	Eldon Miller
Salvatore Ruvolo	Tom Hawkins	George Chaump
Norm McElheney	Dan O'Brien	George O'Leary
Billy O'Brien	Dave O'Brien	Hugh Hindman
Earl Bruce	Jim Anderson	Floyd Stahl
Alex Gibbs	Casey Fredricks	Bill Conley
Terry Forbes	Joe Delamiellure	Glen Mason
Jim Haney	Carl Fanarro	Eric Tudor

The Staff of the USAF Survival School, Fairchild AFB, Washington

Teachers

Bob Barnettson	Prof. Bob Bartells	Prof. Julian Gresser
Prof. William Hubbard	Prof. Roy Lewicki	John Hendrix
Cal Lowery	Don McComas	Dick Stratford
Ernie Reese	Ed Calhoun	William H. Crawford III

Mentors

Prof. Arthur Cullman	David Sandler	Stan McCloy
James Barlow	Wade Stanley	Arthur Jones
Jack Havens	Bob Kanuth	Sonny Spriggs
Ross Bartschy Sr.	Chalmers Wylie	Ron Burson
Art DelNero	James Rhodes	Robert Prescott
Bill Dever	Don Biller	George Castignola
John Easton	Tim McRitchie	Michael Burke

Associates

Phil Kabealo	Bob Jordan	Dick Glenn
Gerry Betterman	Valerie Kosorek	Jack Cowan
Peggy Hunter	Gretchen Shipley	Ross Bartschy Jr.
Dick Butkus	Brian Kelley	R. J. and Lynn
John Barlow	Michael Tobin	Matthew DeLamater

Most important, my thanks to my family for their unwavering support and strength: my wife, Patty; my son Jim and his family—his wife, Cynthia, my grandson, James, and my granddaughter, Jordan; my son Scott and his wife, Meredith; my sons Todd and Brian; and my daughter, Kristina.

Index

About the Author

Jim Camp is a negotiation coach and the founder of Coach2100, Inc., which offers one-on-one coaching to senior managers at corporations as well as group coaching for client teams. He holds annual Negotiator Coach Symposiums and has trained and coached negotiation teams in the United States and throughout the world, on every continent. He has coached people through thousands of negotiations at more than 150 corporations, including Motorola, Texas Instruments, Merrill Lynch, IBM, and Prudential Insurance, as well as many smaller companies in a wide range of industries, including telecommunications, real estate, investment banking, healthcare, import/export, automotive dealers and manufacturers, scientific research labs, and various governmental agencies. Jim has also lectured at various graduate business schools in the United States and has been a featured speaker at *Inc.* magazine's Growing the Company conferences. He is based in Vero Beach, Florida; visit his website: www.Camptraining.com.